GREATEST EVER

Potato

p

This is a Parragon Publishing Book
This edition published in 2003

Parragon Publishing
Queen Street House
4 Queen Street
Bath BA1 1HE, UK

ISBN: 0-75259-948-8

Printed in Dubai

Produced by The Bridgewater Book Company Ltd

NOTE

This book uses metric and imperial measurements. Follow the same units
of measurement throughout; do not mix metric and imperial.
All spoon measurements are level: teaspoons are assumed to be 5 ml,
and tablespoons are assumed to be 15 ml. Unless otherwise stated,
milk is assumed to be full fat, eggs and individual vegetables such as potatoes
are medium, and pepper is freshly ground black pepper.

Recipes using raw or very lightly cooked eggs should be
avoided by infants, the elderly, pregnant women, convalescents, and anyone
suffering from an illness.

Contents

Introduction

The potato is one of the world's most popular vegetables, cultivated in almost every country. There are many different varieties, native to these countries, each having a different quality or property. As a result of this, the potato suits most culinary styles and is  perhaps the most versatile staple food available. It is recognized as one of the most important crops cultivated for human consumption, with Russia, Poland, and Germany being the highest consumers, closely followed by Holland, Cyprus, and Ireland.

We eat about 142 lb/65 kg per head per annum, which is good news when you consider the nutritional properties of this best-loved tuber. A serving of 8 oz/225 g of potatoes contains around 180 calories and provides us with protein, energy-rich starch, and fiber, as well as being a good source of vitamin C. Most of the vitamins are found just beneath the skin, which is why it is often suggested that potatoes are cooked in their skins and then peeled. If not cooked with fat, the potato has a great role to play in the slimming diet, a fact which has been disputed in the past.

Buying and Storing

When choosing potatoes, make sure they are firm and well-shaped with a smooth, tight skin. New potatoes should be eaten as fresh as possible, but old potatoes can be stored in a cool, dark, dry place—exposure to light makes them turn green, resulting in an unpleasant flavor and a higher level of glycoalkaloids, which are naturally occuring toxins.

Preparation and Cooking

To preserve the nutritional value of potatoes, they should be baked in their skins, or scrubbed rather than peeled. If peeled potatoes are required, they should be cooked in their skins and then peeled afterward.

Boiling

For new and old potatoes, place them in a pan, pour in enough boiling water to cover, put on a lid and boil gently until tender.

Steaming

To steam new and old potatoes, place them in a steamer over a pan of boiling water and cook them gently until they are tender.

Mashing or Creaming

Boil the potatoes, then drain well. Add a piece of butter, season, then mash, preferably with an electric hand-whisk, or by hand, first with a potato masher and then stir briskly with a fork. As a variation, add cream or plain yogurt, add a little crème fraîche or fresh pesto sauce.

Roasting

Simmer the potatoes in boiling water for 10 minutes. Drain, then shake them in the pan to roughen their surfaces. Tip carefully into a roasting pan of very hot fat and cook at 220°C/425°F for 45 minutes–1 hour.

Frying

For deep-frying, the temperature of the oil is all-important and a deep-fat fryer is a good investment. Parboiled, sliced or diced potatoes can be sautéd in a little oil in a heavy-based pan.

Baking

Most varieties will bake, but avoid those with thin skins. Scrub and prick the skins, season with salt and bake at 425°F/220°C for 1–1½ hours.

Potato Varieties

There are many varieties of potato, but only about 100 of these are regularly grown. Of these, about 20 are found with ease in our produce stores and supermarkets. The following is a brief description of the most popular varieties and their uses, as a guide for the recipes in this book.

Russet potatoes

Often called old potatoes, or baking potatoes, this is the most popular variety in the US. Russets have rough brown skin and white flesh, which becomes light and fluffy when cooked. They are available year-round and are excellent for baking, mashing, frying, and roasting. Varieties include Russet Burbank, Russet Arcadia, Russet Norkotah, and Butte.

Round White potatoes

This medium-size variety is grown and used most often in the Eastern United States. Also referred to as boiling potatoes, Round Whites have freckled tan skin and white flesh. Their firm, creamy texture when cooked makes this a good, all-purpose variety. They are best for boiling and mashing, and also excellent for roasting and frying.

Round Red potatoes

This variety is available mostly in late summer and early fall. Red potatoes have a rosy red skin and white flesh. They have a firm and moist texture and are best used for salads, roasting, boiling and steaming. Red potatoes are sometimes referred to as "new potatoes," which is technically inaccurate.

Long White potatoes

This variety is long and oval in shape—similar to the Russets. Long White potatoes have thin, light gray-tan skins and few blemishes. They are grown primarily in California and are available in spring through summer. They are sometimes called White Rose or California Long Whites. These all-purpose potatoes have a firm, creamy texture when cooked and can be used in most potato preparations.

Fingerling potatoes

The name given to the small, thumb-size, baby Long White potatoes.

Yellow Flesh potatoes

A variety that is becoming increasingly popular in the United States, although not widely grown. Yukon Gold has a buttery yellow to gold skin and flesh. Its moist texture when boiled makes it perfect for mashing or creaming.

Blue and Purple potatoes

Most available in the fall, this variety has a subtle, nutty flavor and bluish flesh. They are suited best for steaming and baking.

New potatoes

Any freshly dug young potatoes which have not reached maturity. Excellent boiled or pan-roasted whole.

Sweet potatoes and Yams

Sweet potatoes are best fried, boiled or casseroled, and are delicious in spicy dishes. Sweeter yams are best roasted, or mashed in cakes and soufflés.

Soups

Potatoes form the basis of many delicious and easy-to-prepare homemade soups because they are the perfect thickening agent, while adding a subtle flavor. With the addition of just a few ingredients, you can have a selection of soups at your fingertips. Add herbs, onion, garlic, meat, fish, or vegetables, top with herbs or croûtons, and serve with crusty bread for anything from a light appetizer to a filling meal.

potato & mushroom soup

serves four

2 tbsp vegetable oil

1 lb 5 oz/600 g mealy
   potatoes, sliced

1 onion, sliced

2 garlic cloves, crushed

4½ cups beef bouillon

½ cup dried mushrooms, soaked in
   hot water for 20 minutes

2 celery stalks, sliced

2 tbsp brandy

salt and pepper

TOPPING

3 tbsp butter

2 thick slices white bread,
   crusts removed

⅔ cup freshly grated
   Parmesan cheese

TO GARNISH

rehydrated dried mushrooms

1 Heat the vegetable oil in a large
   skillet and add the potato and
onion slices and the garlic. Sauté
gently for 5 minutes, stirring constantly.

2 Add the beef bouillon, dried
   mushrooms and their strained
soaking water, and sliced celery. Bring
to a boil, then reduce the heat to a
simmer, cover the pan, and cook the
soup for 20 minutes, until the potatoes
are tender.

3 Meanwhile, melt the butter for
   the topping in the skillet. Sprinkle
the bread slices with the grated cheese
and cook the slices in the butter for
1 minute on each side, until crisp.
Remove the bread from the skillet and
cut each slice into triangles.

4 Stir the brandy into the soup and
   season to taste. Pour into bowls
and top with the bread. Garnish with
the mushrooms and parsley.

COOK'S TIP

Probably the most popular
dried mushroom is the cep,
but any variety will add a lovely
flavor to this soup. If you do
not wish to use dried
mushrooms, add 1¾ cups sliced
fresh mushrooms of your choice
to the soup.

potato & garbanzo soup

serves four

1 tbsp olive oil

1 large onion, chopped finely

2–3 garlic cloves, chopped finely
    or crushed

1 carrot, sliced thinly

2 cups diced potatoes

¼ tsp ground turmeric

¼ tsp garam masala

¼ tsp mild curry powder

14 oz/400 g canned
    chopped tomatoes

3¾ cups water

¼ tsp chili paste, or to taste

14 oz/400 g canned garbanzo
    beans, drained and rinsed

3 oz/85 g fresh or frozen peas

salt and pepper

chopped fresh cilantro, to garnish

1 Heat the olive oil in a large
    pan over medium heat. Add the
onion and garlic and cook, stirring
occasionally, for 3–4 minutes, until the
onion is beginning to soften.

2 Add the carrot, potatoes,
    turmeric, garam masala, and
curry powder and continue cooking
for 1–2 minutes.

3 Add the tomatoes, measured
    water, and chili paste with a large
pinch of salt. Reduce the heat, then
cover and simmer for 30 minutes,
stirring occasionally.

4 Add the garbanzo beans and
    peas to the pan and continue
cooking for about 15 minutes, or until
all the vegetables are tender.

5 Taste the soup and adjust the
    seasoning, if necessary, adding a
little more chili paste if you like. Ladle
the soup into warm soup bowls,
sprinkle with chopped fresh cilantro,
and serve immediately.

indian potato & pea soup

serves four

2 tbsp vegetable oil

1¼ cups diced mealy potatoes

1 large onion, chopped

2 garlic cloves, crushed

1 tsp garam masala

1 tsp ground coriander

1 tsp ground cumin

3¾ cups vegetable bouillon

1 red chile, seeded
    and chopped

3½ oz/100 g frozen peas

4 tbsp plain yogurt

salt and pepper

chopped fresh cilantro,
    to garnish

warm bread, to serve

1 Heat the vegetable oil in a large pan and add the diced potatoes, onion, and garlic. Cook over low heat, stirring constantly, for about 5 minutes, until the onion is soft.

2 Add the ground spices and cook for 1 minute, stirring constantly.

3 Stir in the vegetable bouillon and chopped red chile and bring the mixture to a boil. Reduce the heat, then cover the pan and simmer for 20 minutes, until the potatoes begin to break down.

4 Add the peas and cook the soup for 5 minutes more. Stir in the yogurt and season to taste with salt and pepper.

5 Pour into warmed soup bowls. Garnish with chopped fresh cilantro and serve immediately with warm bread.

potato & vegetable soup with pistou

serves six

2 young carrots

1 lb/450 g potatoes

7 oz/200 g fresh peas in the pods

7 oz/200 g thin beans

5½ oz/150 g young zucchini

2 tbsp olive oil

1 garlic clove, crushed

1 large onion, chopped finely

10 cups vegetable bouillon or water

1 bouquet garni of 2 fresh parsley
    sprigs and 1 bay leaf tied in a
    3-inch/7.5-cm piece of celery

¾ cup dried small soup pasta

1 large tomato, skinned, seeded,
    and chopped or diced

Parmesan cheese shavings,
    to serve

PISTOU SAUCE

1½ cups fresh basil leaves

1 garlic clove

5 tbsp fruity extra virgin olive oil

salt and pepper

1 To make the pistou sauce, put the basil leaves, garlic, and olive oil in a food processor and process until well blended. Season with salt and pepper to taste. Transfer to a bowl, then cover, and chill until required.

2 Peel the carrots and cut them in half lengthwise, then slice. Peel the potatoes and cut into fourths lengthwise, then slice. Set aside.

3 Shell the peas. Top and tail the beans and cut them into 1-inch/2.5-cm pieces. Cut the zucchini in half lengthwise, then slice.

4 Heat the oil in a large pan or flameproof casserole. Add the garlic and cook for 2 minutes, stirring. Add the onion and continue cooking

for 2 minutes, until soft. Add the carrots and potatoes and stir for about 30 seconds.

5 Pour in the bouillon and bring to a boil. Lower the heat, then partially cover, and simmer for 8 minutes, until the vegetables are starting to become tender.

6 Stir in the peas, beans, zucchini, bouquet garni, pasta, and tomato. Season and cook for about 8–10 minutes, or until tender. Discard the bouquet garni. Stir in the pistou sauce, serve with Parmesan cheese.

leek, potato & bacon soup

serves four

2 tbsp butter

1 cup diced potatoes

4 leeks, shredded

2 garlic cloves, crushed

3½ oz/100 g smoked bacon, diced

3¾ cups vegetable bouillon

1 cup heavy cream

2 tbsp chopped fresh parsley

salt and pepper

TO GARNISH

vegetable oil, for deep-frying

1 leek, shredded

1 Melt the butter in a large pan and add the diced potatoes, shredded leeks, garlic, and diced bacon. Sauté gently for 5 minutes, stirring constantly.

2 Add the vegetable bouillon and bring to a boil. Reduce the heat, then cover the pan and simmer for 20 minutes, until the potatoes are cooked. Stir in the heavy cream.

3 Meanwhile, make the garnish. Half-fill a pan with oil and heat to 350–375°F/180–190°C or until a cube of bread browns in 30 seconds. Add the shredded leek and deep-fry for 1 minute, until browned and crisp, taking care as it contains water. Drain the shredded leek thoroughly on paper towels and reserve.

4 Reserve a few pieces of potato, leek, and bacon and set aside. Put the rest of the soup in a food processor or blender, in batches, and process each batch for 30 seconds. Return the puréed soup to a clean pan and heat through.

5 Stir in the reserved vegetables, bacon, and parsley and season to taste. Pour into warmed bowls and garnish with the fried leeks.

VARIATION

For a lighter soup, omit the cream and stir yogurt or skim milk into the soup at the end of the cooking time.

chicken & vegetable soup

serves four

4 cups chicken bouillon

6 oz/175 g skinless, boneless
   chicken breast portions

fresh parsley and tarragon sprigs

2 garlic cloves, crushed

4½ oz/125 g baby carrots, halved or
   quartered

8 oz/225 g small new potatoes,
   quartered

4 tbsp all-purpose flour

½ cup milk

4–5 scallions, diagonally sliced

3 oz/85 g asparagus tips, halved
   and cut into 1½-inch/4-cm pieces

½ cup heavy cream

1 tbsp chopped finely fresh parsley

1 tbsp chopped finely fresh tarragon

salt and pepper

1 Put the bouillon in a pan with the chicken, parsley and tarragon sprigs, and garlic. Bring just to a boil, then reduce the heat, cover, and simmer for 20 minutes, or until the chicken is cooked through and firm to the touch.

2 Remove the chicken and strain the bouillon. When the chicken is cool enough to handle, cut into bite-size pieces.

3 Return the bouillon to the pan and bring to a boil. Adjust the heat so the liquid boils very gently. Add the carrots, cover, and cook for 5 minutes. Add the potatoes, cover again, and cook for about 12 minutes, or until all the vegetables are beginning to become tender.

4 Meanwhile, put the flour in a small mixing bowl and very slowly whisk in the milk to make a thick paste. Pour in a little of the hot bouillon mixture and stir to make a smooth liquid.

5 Stir the flour mixture into the soup and bring just to a boil, stirring. Boil gently for 4–5 minutes, until it thickens, stirring frequently.

6 Add the scallions, asparagus, and chicken. Reduce the heat a little and simmer for about 15 minutes, until all the vegetables are tender. Stir in the cream and herbs. Season and serve.

spinach & ginger soup

serves four

2 tbsp sunflower oil

1 onion, chopped

2 garlic cloves, chopped finely

2 tsp fresh gingerroot, chopped
   finely

4 cups fresh young spinach leaves

1 small lemongrass stem,
   chopped finely

4 cups chicken or vegetable bouillon

8 oz/225 g potato, peeled
   and chopped

1 tbsp rice wine or dry sherry

1 tsp sesame oil

salt and pepper

1 Heat the oil in a large pan. Add the onion, garlic, and ginger and cook gently for 3–4 minutes, until softened but not browned.

2 Reserve 2–3 small spinach leaves. Add the remaining leaves and lemongrass to the pan, stirring until the spinach is wilted. Add the bouillon and potato to the pan and bring to a boil. Lower the heat, cover, and simmer for about 10 minutes.

3 Tip the soup into a blender or food processor and process until completely smooth.

4 Return the soup to the pan and add the rice wine or sherry, then adjust the seasoning to taste. Heat until just about to boil.

5 Finely shred the 2–3 reserved spinach leaves and sprinkle some over the top. Drizzle with a few drops of sesame oil. Ladle the soup into warm soup bowls and serve immediately, garnished with the remaining finely shredded leaves.

COOK'S TIP

To make a creamy-textured spinach and coconut soup, stir in about 4 tablespoons coconut cream, or alternatively replace about 1 ¼ cups of the bouillon with coconut milk (both available from Asian supermarkets). Serve the soup with shavings of fresh coconut sprinkled over the surface.

potato & split pea soup

serves four

2 tbsp vegetable oil

2⅔ cups diced mealy
    potatoes, unpeeled

2 onions, diced

2¾ oz/75 g split green peas

4½ cups vegetable bouillon

¾ cup grated Swiss cheese

salt and pepper

CROUTONS

3 tbsp butter

1 garlic clove, crushed

1 tbsp chopped fresh parsley

1 thick slice white bread, diced

1 Heat the vegetable oil in a large pan. Add the potatoes and onions and sauté over low heat, stirring constantly, for about 5 minutes.

2 Add the split green peas to the pan and stir well to mix together.

3 Pour the vegetable bouillon into the pan and bring to a boil. Reduce the heat to low and simmer for 35 minutes, until the potatoes are tender and the split peas cooked.

4 Meanwhile, make the croûtons. Melt the butter in a skillet. Add the garlic, parsley, and bread cubes and cook, turning frequently, for about 2 minutes, until the bread cubes are golden brown on all sides.

5 Stir the grated Swiss cheese into the soup and season to taste with salt and pepper. Heat gently until the cheese is just starting to melt. Pour the soup into warmed individual bowls and sprinkle the croûtons on top, then serve immediately.

lentil, potato & ham soup

serves five

10½ oz/300 g Puy lentils

2 tsp butter

1 large onion, chopped finely

2 carrots, chopped finely

1 garlic clove,
  chopped finely

2 cups water

1 bay leaf

¼ tsp dried sage or rosemary

4 cups chicken bouillon

1⅓ cup finely diced potatoes

1 tbsp tomato paste

⅔ cup finely diced
  smoked ham

salt and pepper

chopped fresh parsley,
  to garnish

1 Rinse the lentils under cold running water, drain and pick over to check for any small stones.

2 Melt the butter in a large pan or flameproof casserole over medium heat. Add the onion, carrots, and garlic, then cover and cook, stirring frequently, for 4–5 minutes, until the onion is slightly softened but not colored.

3 Add the lentils to the vegetables with the measured water, bay leaf, and sage or rosemary. Bring to a boil, then reduce the heat, cover, and simmer for 10 minutes.

4 Add the bouillon, potatoes, tomato paste, and ham. Bring back to a simmer. Cover and continue simmering for 25–30 minutes, or until the vegetables are tender.

5 Season to taste with salt and pepper and remove the bay leaf. Ladle into warm bowls, then garnish with parsley and serve.

broccoli & potato soup

serves four

2 tbsp olive oil

2⅔ cups diced potatoes

1 onion, diced

8 oz/225 g broccoli flowerets

4½ oz/125 g blue cheese, crumbled

4½ cups vegetable bouillon

⅔ cup heavy cream

pinch of paprika

salt and pepper

COOK'S TIP

This soup freezes very successfully. Follow the method described here up to step 4 and freeze the soup after it has been processed. Add the cream and paprika just before serving. Garnish and serve.

VARIATION

This soup also tastes delicious made with grated sharp Cheddar instead of blue cheese.

1 Heat the oil in a large pan and add the potatoes and onion. Sauté, stirring, for 5 minutes.

2 Reserve a few broccoli flowerets for the garnish and add the remainder to the pan. Add the cheese and bouillon.

3 Bring to a boil, then reduce the heat, cover the pan, and simmer gently for 25 minutes, until the potatoes are tender.

4 Transfer the soup to a food processor or blender, in batches, and process until the mixture is a smooth purée.

5 Return the purée to a clean pan and stir in the cream and a pinch of paprika. Season to taste with salt and pepper.

6 Blanch the reserved broccoli flowerets in a little boiling water for about 2 minutes, then drain with a slotted spoon.

7 Pour the soup into warmed bowls and garnish with the broccoli flowerets and a sprinkling of paprika. Serve immediately.

fava bean & mint soup

serves four

2 tbsp olive oil

1 red onion, chopped

2 garlic cloves, crushed

2⅔ cups diced potatoes

3 cups fava beans, thawed if frozen

3¾ cups vegetable bouillon

2 tbsp freshly chopped mint

plain yogurt and fresh mint sprigs,
    to garnish

1 Heat the olive oil in a large pan. Add the onion and garlic and sauté for 2–3 minutes, until softened.

2 Add the potatoes and cook, stirring constantly, for 5 minutes.

3 Stir in the beans and the bouillon. Cover and simmer gently for 30 minutes, or until the beans and potatoes are tender.

4 Remove a few vegetables with a slotted spoon and set aside. Place the remainder of the soup in a food processor or blender and process to a smooth purée.

5 Return the soup to a clean pan and add the reserved vegetables and chopped mint. Stir thoroughly and heat through gently.

6 Ladle the soup into a warm tureen or individual serving bowls. Garnish with swirls of plain yogurt and sprigs of fresh mint and serve immediately.

roasted garlic & potato soup

serves four

1 large bulb of garlic with large
   cloves, peeled (about 3½ oz/
   100 g)
2 tsp olive oil, plus extra for
   brushing
2 large leeks, sliced thinly
1 large onion, chopped finely
1 lb 2 oz/500 g potatoes, diced
5 cups vegetable bouillon
1 bay leaf
⅔ cup light cream
freshly grated nutmeg
fresh lemon juice (optional)
salt and pepper
TO GARNISH
chopped fresh chives or parsley
sprinkle of paprika

1 Put the garlic cloves in an ovenproof dish. Lightly brush with oil and bake in a preheated oven, 350°F/180°C for about 20 minutes, until golden.

2 Heat the oil in a large pan over medium heat. Add the leeks and onion, then cover and cook for about 3 minutes, stirring frequently, until they begin to soften.

3 Add the potatoes, roasted garlic, bouillon, and bay leaf. Season with salt (unless the bouillon is salty) and pepper. Bring to a boil, reduce the heat, cover, and cook gently for about 30 minutes, until the vegetables are tender. Remove the bay leaf.

4 Let the soup cool slightly, then transfer to a blender or food processor and process until smooth, working in batches if necessary. (If using a food processor, strain off the cooking liquid and reserve. Process the soup solids with enough cooking liquid to moisten them, then combine with the remaining liquid.)

5 Return the soup to the pan and stir in the cream and a generous grating of nutmeg. Taste and adjust the seasoning, if necessary, adding a few drops of lemon juice, if wished. Reheat over a low heat. Ladle into warm soup bowls, then garnish with chives or parsley and paprika and serve.

25

sweet potato & apple soup

serves six

1 tbsp butter

3 leeks, sliced thinly

1 large carrot, sliced thinly

1 lb 5 oz/600 g sweet potatoes,
   peeled and diced

2 large tart eating apples, peeled
   and diced

5 cups water

freshly grated nutmeg

1 cup apple juice

1 cup light cream

salt and pepper

chopped fresh chives or cilantro, to
   garnish

1 Melt the butter in a large pan over medium-low heat. Add the leeks, then cover and cook, stirring frequently, for 6–8 minutes, or until softened but not colored.

2 Add the carrot, sweet potatoes, apples, and water. Season lightly with salt, pepper, and nutmeg. Bring to a boil, then reduce the heat, cover and simmer, stirring occasionally, for about 20 minutes, until the vegetables are very tender.

3 Let the soup cool slightly, then transfer to a blender or food processor, and process until smooth, working in batches if necessary. (If using a food processor, strain off the cooking liquid and reserve. Process the soup solids with enough cooking liquid to moisten them, then combine with the remaining liquid.)

4 Return the soup to the pan and stir in the apple juice. Place over low heat and simmer for about 10 minutes, until heated through.

5 Stir in the cream and continue simmering for about 5 minutes, stirring frequently, until heated through. Taste and adjust the seasoning, adding more salt, pepper, and nutmeg, if necessary. Ladle the soup into warm bowls, then garnish with a swirl of cream, sprinkle with chives or cilantro, and serve.

celery root, leek & potato soup

serves four

1 tbsp butter

1 onion, chopped

2 large leeks, halved lengthwise
and sliced

1 large celery root, peeled
and diced

8 oz/225 g potatoes, diced

1 carrot, quartered and sliced thinly

5 cups water

pinch of dried marjoram

1 bay leaf

freshly grated nutmeg

salt and pepper

celery leaves, to garnish

1 Melt the butter in a large pan
over medium–low heat. Add the
onion and leeks and cook, stirring
occasionally, for about 4 minutes, until
just softened and translucent but
not colored.

2 Add the celery root, potato,
carrot, water, marjoram, and
bay leaf, with a large pinch of salt.
Bring to a boil, then reduce the heat,
cover and simmer gently for about
25 minutes, until the vegetables are
tender. Remove the bay leaf.

3 Let the soup cool slightly. Transfer
to a blender or food processor
and process until smooth. (If using a
food processor, strain off the cooking
liquid and reserve. Process the soup
solids with enough cooking liquid to
moisten them, then combine with the
remaining liquid.)

4 Return the puréed soup to the
pan and stir to blend. Season to
taste with salt, pepper, and grated
nutmeg. Simmer gently over medium–
low heat for a few minutes, until
heated through.

5 Ladle the soup into warm serving
bowls. Garnish with celery leaves
and serve immediately.

vegetable & corn chowder

serves four

1 tbsp vegetable oil

1 red onion, diced

1 red bell pepper, seeded
  and diced

3 garlic cloves, crushed

1¼ cups diced potatoes

2 tbsp all-purpose flour

2½ cups milk

1¼ cups vegetable bouillon

1¾ oz/50 g broccoli flowerets

3 cups canned corn, drained

¾ cup grated Cheddar cheese

salt and pepper

1 tbsp chopped cilantro,
  to garnish

COOK'S TIP

Vegetarian cheeses are made
with rennets of non-animal
origin, using microbial or
fungal enzymes.

1 Heat the oil in a large pan. Add the onion, bell pepper, garlic, and potato and sauté over low heat, stirring frequently, for 2–3 minutes, until the onion is softened and translucent but not colored.

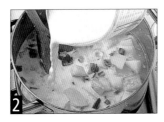

2 Stir in the flour and cook, stirring constantly for about 30 seconds. Gradually stir in the milk and bouillon until smooth.

3 Add the broccoli and corn. Bring the mixture to a boil, stirring constantly, then reduce the heat and simmer for about 20 minutes, or until all the vegetables are tender.

4 Add ½ cup of the cheese and stir until it melts.

5 Season to taste with salt and pepper and spoon the chowder into a warm soup tureen. Garnish with the remaining cheese and the chopped cilantro and serve.

green soup

serves four

1 tbsp olive oil

1 onion, chopped

1 garlic clove, chopped

7 oz/200 g potato, cut into 1-inch/
    2.5-cm cubes

3 cups vegetable or chicken bouillon

1 small cucumber or ½ large
    cucumber, cut into chunks

3 oz/85 g watercress

4½ oz/125 g green beans, trimmed
    and halved lengthwise

salt and pepper

VARIATION

Substitute 1½ cups snow peas
for the beans, and spinach for
the watercress.

COOK'S TIP

The most suitable olive oil for
cooking is virgin oil. "Pure" oil is
highly refined and likely to have
been heat treated.

---

1 Heat the olive oil in a large, heavy pan. Add the onion and garlic and cook over medium heat, stirring occasionally, for 3–4 minutes, or until softened but not coloured.

2 Add the potato cubes and cook for 2–3 minutes more. Stir in the bouillon and bring to a boil. Lower the heat and simmer for 5 minutes.

3 Add the cucumber to the pan and cook for 3 minutes more, or until the potatoes are tender. Test by inserting the tip of a sharp knife into the potato cubes—it should pass through easily.

4 Add the watercress and cook until just wilted. Remove from heat and set aside to cool slightly, then transfer to a food processor, and process to a smooth purée. Alternatively, before adding the watercress, mash the vegetables with a potato masher and push through a strainer, then chop the watercress finel, and stir into the soup.

5 Bring a small pan of water to a boil and steam the beans for 3–4 minutes, or until tender. Add the beans to the soup, season to taste with salt and pepper, and warm through. Ladle into warmed soup bowls and serve immediately. Alternatively, set aside to cool and then chill.

carrot & cumin soup

serves four–six

3 tbsp butter or margarine

1 large onion, chopped

1–2 garlic cloves, crushed

12 oz/350 g carrots, sliced

3¼ cups chicken or vegetable
  bouillon

¾ tsp ground cumin

2 celery stalks, sliced thinly

4 oz/115 g potato, diced

2 tsp tomato paste

2 tsp lemon juice

2 fresh or dried bay leaves

about 1¼ cups skim milk

salt and pepper

celery leaves, to garnish

1 Melt the butter or margarine in a large pan. Add the onion and garlic and cook very gently until softened but not colored.

2 Add the carrots and cook over low heat for 5 minutes more, stirring frequently and taking care they do not brown.

3 Add the bouillon, cumin, seasoning, celery, potato, tomato paste, lemon juice, and bay leaves and bring to a boil. Cover and simmer for about 30 minutes, until all the vegetables are tender.

4 Remove and discard the bay leaves, cool the soup a little, and then press it through a strainer, or process in a food processor or blender until smooth.

5 Pour the soup into a clean pan, add the milk, and bring to a boil over low heat. Taste and adjust the seasoning if necessary.

6 Ladle into warmed bowls, garnish each serving with a small celery leaf, and serve.

COOK'S TIP

This soup can be frozen for up to 3 months. Add the milk when reheating.

sweet potato & squash soup

serves six

12 oz/350 g sweet potatoes

1 acorn squash

4 shallots

olive oil, for brushing

5–6 garlic cloves, unpeeled

3¾ cups chicken bouillon

½ cup light cream

salt and pepper

chopped fresh chives, to garnish

1 Cut the sweet potato, squash, and shallots in half lengthwise. Brush the cut sides with oil.

2 Put the vegetables, cut sides down, in a shallow roasting pan. Add the garlic cloves. Roast in a preheated oven, 375°F/190°C for about 40 minutes, until tender and light brown. Remove the pan from the oven and set aside to cool.

3 When cool, scoop the flesh from the potato and squash halves, and put in a pan with the shallots. Squeeze out the soft insides from the garlic and add to the other vegetables.

4 Add the bouillon and a pinch of salt. Bring to a boil, then reduce the heat and simmer, partially covered, for 30 minutes, stirring occasionally, until the vegetables are very tender.

5 Let the soup cool slightly, then transfer to a blender or food processor and process until smooth. (If using a food processor, strain off the cooking liquid and reserve. Process the soup solids with enough cooking liquid to moisten them, then combine with the remaining liquid.)

6 Return the soup to the pan and stir in the cream. Season to taste, then simmer for 5–10 minutes, until heated through. Serve immediately.

watercress vichyssoise

serves six

1 tbsp olive oil

3 large leeks, sliced thinly

2 cups potatoes, diced finely

2½ cups chicken or
    vegetable bouillon

2 cups water

1 bay leaf

6 oz/175g prepared watercress

¾ cup light cream

salt and pepper

watercress leaves, to garnish

1 Heat the oil in a large, heavy pan over medium heat. Add the leeks and cook for about 3 minutes, stirring frequently, until they begin to soften but not color.

COOK'S TIP

For garlic croûtons, cut off the crusts from 3 slices of day-old bread, then cut the bread into ¼-inch/5-mm dice. Heat 3 tablespoons olive oil in a skillet and stir-fry 1 chopped large garlic clove for 2 minutes, then remove. Fry the diced bread until golden all over. Drain well.

2 Add the potatoes, bouillon, measured water, and bay leaf. Add salt if the bouillon is unsalted. Bring to a boil, then reduce the heat, cover, and cook gently for about 25 minutes, until all the vegetables are tender. Remove the bay leaf.

3 Add the watercress and continue to cook, stirring frequently, for 2–3 minutes more, until the watercress is completely wilted.

4 Let the soup cool slightly, then transfer to a blender or food processor and process until smooth, working in batches if necessary. (If using a food processor, strain off the cooking liquid and reserve. Process the soup solids with enough cooking liquid to moisten them, then combine with the remaining liquid.)

5 Put the soup in a large bowl and stir in half the cream. Taste and season with salt, if necessary, and plenty of pepper. Cover the bowl with plastic wrap and let cool.

6 Chill until cold. Taste and adjust the seasoning, if necessary. Ladle into chilled bowls, then drizzle the remaining cream on top and garnish with watercress leaves. Serve the watercress vichyssoise immediately.

minted pea & yogurt soup

serves six

2 tbsp vegetable ghee or
    sunflower oil
2 onions, chopped coarsely
8 oz/225 g potato, chopped
    coarsely
2 garlic cloves
1-inch/2.5-cm piece of
    gingerroot, chopped
1 tsp ground coriander
1 tsp ground cumin
1 tbsp all-purpose flour
3¾ cups vegetable bouillon
4½ cups frozen peas
2–3 tbsp chopped fresh mint
⅔ cups strained plain yogurt, plus
    extra to garnish
½ tsp cornstarch
1¼ cups milk
salt and pepper
fresh mint sprigs, to garnish

1 Heat the vegetable ghee or sunflower oil in a large pan, add the onions and potato and cook over low heat, stirring occasionally, for about 3–5 minutes, until the onion is softened and translucent but not colored.

2 Stir in the garlic, ginger, coriander, cumin, and flour and cook, stirring constantly, for 1 minute.

3 Add the vegetable bouillon, peas, and half the mint and bring to a boil, stirring constantly. Reduce the heat to very low, cover and simmer gently for 15 minutes, or until the vegetables are tender.

4 Process the soup, in batches, in a blender or food processor. Return the mixture to the pan and season with salt and pepper to taste. Blend the yogurt with the cornstarch to a smooth paste and stir into the soup.

5 Add the milk and bring almost to a boil, stirring constantly. Cook very gently for 2 minutes. Serve hot, garnished with small mint sprigs and a swirl of extra yogurt.

vichyssoise

serves six

3 large leeks

3 tbsp butter or margarine

1 onion, sliced thinly

1 lb 2 oz/500 g potatoes, chopped

3½ cups vegetable bouillon

2 tsp lemon juice

pinch of grated nutmeg

¼ tsp ground coriander

1 bay leaf

1 egg yolk

⅔ cup light cream

salt and white pepper

chopped fresh chives, to garnish

1 Trim the leeks and remove most of the green part. Slice the white part of the leeks very thinly.

2 Melt the butter or margarine in a pan. Add the leeks and onion and cook, stirring occasionally, for about 5 minutes without browning.

3 Add the potatoes, vegetable bouillon, lemon juice, grated nutmeg, coriander, and bay leaf to the pan. Season to taste with salt and pepper and bring to a boil. Cover and simmer over low heat, stirring occasionally, for about 30 minutes, until all the vegetables are very soft.

4 Cool the soup a little. Remove and discard the bay leaf and then press through a strainer or process in a food processor or blender until smooth. Pour into a clean pan.

5 Blend the egg yolk into the cream. Add a little of the soup to this mixture and then whisk it all back into the soup. Reheat gently, without boiling. Adjust the seasoning to taste. Cover with plastic wrap, cool, and then chill thoroughly in the refrigerator.

6 Serve the soup sprinkled with chopped fresh chives.

fennel & tomato soup

serves four

2 tsp olive oil

1 large onion, halved and sliced

2 large fennel bulbs, halved
   and sliced

1 small potato, diced

3¾ cups water

1⅔ cups tomato juice

1 bay leaf

4½ oz/125 g cooked peeled
   small shrimp

2 tomatoes, skinned, seeded,
   and chopped

½ tsp chopped fresh dill

salt and pepper

fresh dill sprigs or fennel fronds,
   to garnish

COOK'S TIP

When buying fennel, look for
well-rounded, plump bulbs with
no signs of bruising or
discoloration. The bulbs should
be dry, but not dried out.

1 Heat the olive oil in a large, heavy
pan over medium heat. Add the
sliced onion and fennel and cook for
3–4 minutes, stirring occasionally,
until the onion is just softened and
translucent but not colored.

2 Add the potato, water, tomato
juice, and bay leaf with a large
pinch of salt. Reduce the heat, then
cover and simmer gently for about
25 minutes, stirring once or twice, until
the vegetables are soft.

3 Let cool slightly, then transfer to a
blender or food processor. Process
until smooth, working in batches if
necessary. (If using a food processor,
strain off the cooking liquid and
reserve. Process the solids with enough
cooking liquid to moisten them, then
mix with the remaining liquid.)

4 Return the soup to the pan and
add the shrimp. Simmer gently
over low heat, stirring occasionally, for
about 10 minutes, to reheat the soup
and let it fully absorb the flavor of
the shrimp.

5 Stir in the tomatoes and dill. Taste
and adjust the seasoning, adding
salt, if needed, and pepper. Thin the
soup with a little more tomato juice if
you like. Ladle into warm bowls, then
garnish with dill or fennel fronds and
serve immediately.

new england clam chowder

serves four

2 lb/900 g live clams

4 rindless lean bacon
  strips, chopped

2 tbsp butter

1 onion, chopped

1 tbsp chopped fresh thyme

1¾ cups diced potato

1¼ cups milk

1 bay leaf

1⅔ cups heavy cream

1 tbsp chopped fresh parsley

salt and pepper

fresh thyme sprig, to garnish

1 Scrub the clams and put into a large pan with a splash of water. Cook over high heat for 3–4 minutes, until all the clams have opened. Discard any that remain closed. Strain the clams, reserving the cooking liquid. Set aside until cool enough to handle.

2 Reserve 8 of the clams for the garnish. Remove the remainder from their shells. Chop coarsely if large.

3 In a clean pan, cook the bacon until browned and crisp. Drain on paper towels. Add the butter to the same pan and when it has melted, add the onion. Cook for 4–5 minutes, until softened but not colored. Add the

thyme and cook briefly before adding the diced potato, reserved clam cooking liquid, milk, and bay leaf. Bring to a boil and simmer gently for 10 minutes, until the potato is tender but not falling apart. Remove and discard the bay leaf.

4 Transfer to a food processor and process until smooth, or push through a strainer into a bowl with the back of a spoon.

5 Add the reserved clams, bacon, and the cream. Simmer for 2–3 minutes more, until heated through. Season to taste. Stir in the chopped parsley, garnish and serve.

smoked haddock soup

serves four

1 tbsp vegetable oil

2 oz/55 g bacon, cut into
  thin strips

1 large onion, chopped finely

2 tbsp all-purpose flour

4 cups milk

1 lb 9 oz/700 g potatoes, diced

6 oz/175 g skinless smoked
  haddock fillet

salt and pepper

finely chopped fresh parsley,
  to garnish

COOK'S TIP

Cutting the potatoes into small
cubes not only looks attractive,
but lets them cook more quickly
and evenly.

1 Heat the oil in a large pan over medium heat. Add the bacon and cook for 2 minutes. Stir in the onion and continue cooking for 5–7 minutes, stirring frequently, until the onion is soft and the bacon golden. Tip the pan gently and carefully spoon off as much fat as possible.

2 Stir in the flour and continue cooking, stirring constantly, for 2 minutes. Add half of the milk and stir well, scraping the base of the pan to mix in the flour.

3 Add the potatoes and remaining milk and season with pepper. Bring just to a boil, stirring frequently, then reduce the heat and simmer, partially covered, for 10 minutes.

4 Add the fish and continue cooking, stirring occasionally, for about 15 minutes, or until the potatoes are done and the fish is tender and breaks up easily.

5 Taste the soup and adjust the seasoning (salt may not be needed.) Ladle into a warm tureen or bowls and sprinkle generously with chopped parsley.

41

bouillabaisse

serves six

1 lb/450 g jumbo shrimp

1 lb 10 oz/750 g firm white fish
   fillets, such as sea bass, snapper,
   and monkfish

4 tbsp olive oil

grated rind of 1 orange

1 large garlic clove, chopped finely

½ tsp chili paste or harissa

1 large leek, sliced

1 onion, halved and sliced

1 red bell pepper, seeded
   and sliced

4 tomatoes, cored and cut into 8

4 garlic cloves, sliced

1 bay leaf

pinch of saffron threads

½ tsp fennel seeds

2½ cups water

5 cups fish bouillon

1 fennel bulb, chopped finely

1 large onion, chopped finely

8 oz/225 g potatoes, halved and
   sliced thinly

9 oz/250 g scallops

salt and pepper

TO SERVE

ready-made aïoli

toasted French bread slices

dill sprigs, to garnish

1 Peel the shrimp and reserve the shells. Cut the fish into pieces 2 inches/5 cm square. Trim any ragged edges and reserve. Put the fish in a bowl with 2 tablespoons of the olive oil, the orange rind, crushed garlic, and chili paste or harissa. Turn to coat, cover and chill the shrimp and fish separately in the refrigerator.

2 Heat 1 tablespoon of the olive oil in a large pan over medium heat. Add the leek, onion, and red bell pepper. Cook, stirring frequently, for 5 minutes, until the onion softens.

3 Stir in the tomatoes, sliced garlic, bay leaf, saffron, fennel seeds, shrimp shells, water, and fish bouillon. Bring to a boil, reduce the heat and simmer, covered, for 30 minutes. Strain well.

4 Heat the remaining oil in a large pan. Add the fennel and onion and cook, stirring frequently, for about 4–5 minutes, until the onion softens. Add the bouillon and potatoes and bring to a boil. Reduce the heat slightly, cover and cook for 12–15 minutes, or until the potatoes are just tender.

5 Reduce the heat to a simmer and add the fish, starting with the thicker pieces and adding the thinner ones after 2–3 minutes. Add the shrimp and scallops and simmer until all the fish is cooked and opaque.

6 Taste the soup and adjust the seasoning. Spread the aïoli on the toasted bread slices and arrange on top of the soup. Garnish and serve.

COOK'S TIP

There are as many versions of bouillabaisse as there are villages on the French Mediterranean coast. You can use whichever fish you like, but choose thick fillets with firm flesh.

Salads, Appetizers, & Light Meals

Potatoes are very versatile and can be used as a base to create an array of tempting light meals. They are also nutritious, and their carbohydrate gives a welcome energy boost. As potatoes have a fairly neutral flavor, they can be teamed with a variety of other ingredients and flavors.

Also featured in this chapter are appetizers and salads based on potatoes. In addition to the creamy potato salads that are so popular, there are many other recipes to tempt your palate, including dishes suitable for light lunches. Many are also ideal for barbecues and picnics.

nests of chinese salad

serves four

POTATO NESTS

2¼ cups grated mealy potatoes

1 cup cornstarch

vegetable oil, for deep-frying

fresh chives, to garnish

SALAD

4½ oz/125 g pineapple, diced

1 green bell pepper, seeded and cut
  into strips

1 carrot, cut into thin strips

1¾ oz/50 g snow peas,
  sliced thickly

4 baby corn cobs, halved lengthwise

¼ cup bean sprouts

2 scallions, sliced

DRESSING

1 tbsp honey

1 tsp light soy sauce

1 garlic clove, crushed

1 tsp lemon juice

COOK'S TIP

A wok is ideal for cooking the
nests, as there is plenty of room,
but you could use a large skillet.

1 To make the nests, rinse the
potatoes several times in cold
water. Drain well on paper towels so
that they are completely dry. This is to
prevent the potatoes from spitting
when they are cooked in the oil. Place
the potatoes in a large mixing bowl.
Add the cornstarch, mixing well to coat
the potatoes.

2 Half fill a wok with vegetable oil
and heat until smoking. Line a
6-inch/15-cm diameter wire strainer
with a quarter of the potato mixture
and press another strainer of the same
size on top.

3 Lower the strainers into the oil
and cook for 2 minutes, until the
potato nest is golden brown and crisp.
Remove from the wok, and drain well
on paper towels.

4 Repeat 3 more times, to use up
all of the mixture and make a
total of 4 nests. Let cool.

5 Combine all the salad ingredients,
then spoon the salad into the
potato baskets.

6 Combine the dressing ingredients.
Pour the dressing over the salad.
Garnish with fresh chives and then
serve immediately.

beet salad & dill dressing

serves four

2⅔ cups diced waxy potatoes

4 small cooked beets, sliced

½ small cucumber, sliced thinly

2 large dill pickles, sliced

1 red onion, halved and sliced

fresh dill sprigs, to garnish

DRESSING

1 garlic clove, crushed

2 tbsp olive oil

2 tbsp red wine vinegar

2 tbsp chopped fresh dill

salt and pepper

1 Cook the potatoes in a pan of boiling water for 15 minutes, or until tender. Drain and leave to cool.

2 When cool, combine the potato and beets in a large bowl and set aside until required.

3 Line a large salad platter with the slices of cucumber, dill pickles, and red onion.

4 Carefully spoon the potato and beet mixture into the center of the platter.

5 In a small bowl, whisk all the dressing ingredients together, then pour over the salad.

6 Serve the potato and beet salad immediately, garnished with fresh dill sprigs.

broiled new potato salad

serves four

1½ lb/675 g new
  potatoes, scrubbed

3 tbsp olive oil

2 tbsp chopped fresh thyme

1 tsp paprika

4 smoked bacon strips

salt and pepper

fresh parsley sprig, to garnish

DRESSING

4 tbsp mayonnaise

1 tbsp garlic wine vinegar

2 garlic cloves, crushed

1 tbsp chopped fresh parsley

1 Cook the new potatoes in a large pan of boiling water for about 10 minutes, until tender. Drain well and turn into a bowl.

2 Combine the olive oil, chopped thyme, and paprika, and pour the mixture over the warm potatoes, tossing gently to coat.

3 Place the bacon strips under a preheated medium broiler and cook, turning once, for 5 minutes, until crisp. When cooked, coarsely chop the bacon and keep warm.

4 Transfer the potatoes to the broiler pan and cook for 10 minutes, turning once.

5 Combine all the dressing ingredients in a small serving bowl. Transfer the potatoes and bacon to a large serving bowl. Season to taste with salt and pepper and mix together thoroughly.

6 Spoon over the dressing. Garnish with a parsley sprig and serve immediately for a warm salad. Alternatively, let cool and serve chilled.

indian potato salad

serves four

generous 5 cups diced mealy potatoes

2¾ oz/75 g small broccoli flowerets

1 small mango, diced

4 scallions, sliced

salt and pepper

small cooked spiced poppadoms,
    to serve

DRESSING

½ tsp ground cumin

½ tsp ground coriander

1 tbsp mango chutney

⅔ cup low-fat plain yogurt

1 tsp chopped fresh gingerroot

2 tbsp chopped fresh cilantro

1 Cook the potatoes in a large pan of boiling water for 10 minutes, or until tender. Drain well and place in a mixing bowl.

2 Meanwhile, blanch the broccoli flowerets in a separate pan of boiling water for 2 minutes. Drain the broccoli well and add to the potatoes in the bowl.

3 When the potatoes and broccoli have cooled, add the diced mango and sliced scallions. Season to taste with salt and pepper and mix well to combine.

4 In a small bowl, stir all of the dressing ingredients together.

5 Spoon the dressing over the potato mixture and mix together carefully, taking care not to break up the potatoes and broccoli.

6 Serve the salad immediately, accompanied by the small cooked spiced poppadoms.

mexican potato salad

serves four

2 lb 12 oz/1.25 kg waxy
potatoes, sliced
1 ripe avocado
1 tsp olive oil
1 tsp lemon juice
1 garlic clove, crushed
1 onion, chopped
2 large tomatoes, sliced
1 fresh green chile, seeded
and chopped
1 yellow bell pepper, seeded and
sliced
2 tbsp chopped fresh cilantro
salt and pepper
lemon wedges, to garnish

3 Add the olive oil, lemon juice,
garlic, and chopped onion to the
avocado flesh and stir to mix. Cover
the bowl with plastic wrap, to
minimize discoloration, and set aside.

4 Combine the tomatoes, green
chile, and yellow bell pepper and
transfer to a salad bowl with the
potato slices.

5 Arrange the avocado mixture on
top of the salad and sprinkle with
the chopped fresh cilantro. Season to
taste with salt and pepper and serve
the salad immediately, garnished with
lemon wedges.

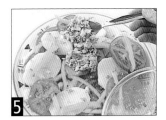

1 Cook the potato slices in a pan of
boiling water for 10–15 minutes,
or until tender. Drain and let cool.

2 Meanwhile, cut the avocado in
half, remove the pit and peel.
Mash the avocado flesh with a fork
(you could also scoop the avocado
flesh from the 2 halves using a spoon
and then mash it).

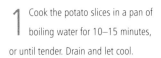

sweet potato salad

serves four

2¼ cups diced sweet potatoes

4 tbsp butter

1 tbsp lemon juice

1 garlic clove, crushed

1 red bell pepper, seeded and diced

1 green bell pepper, seeded
    and diced

2 bananas, sliced thickly

2 thick slices white bread, crusts
    removed, diced

salt and pepper

DRESSING

2 tbsp honey

2 tbsp chopped fresh chives

2 tbsp lemon juice

2 tbsp olive oil

COOK'S TIP

Use firm, slightly underripe
bananas in this recipe as they
won't turn soft and mushy
when they are cooked.

1 Cook the sweet potatoes in a
large pan of boiling water for
10–15 minutes, until tender. Drain
thoroughly and set aside.

2 Meanwhile, melt the butter in
a skillet. Add the lemon juice,
garlic, and bell peppers and cook,
stirring constantly, for 3 minutes.

3 Add the bananas to the skillet
and cook for 1 minute. Remove
the bananas from the pan with a slotted
spoon and stir into the potatoes.

4 Add the bread cubes to the skillet
and cook, stirring frequently, for
2 minutes, until they are golden brown
on all sides.

5 Mix the dressing ingredients
together in a small pan and heat
until well combined.

6 Spoon the potato mixture into a
serving dish and season to taste
with salt and pepper. Pour the dressing
over the potatoes and sprinkle the
croûtons over the top. Serve the sweet
potato salad immediately.

potato salad

serves four

1 lb 9 oz/700 g tiny new potatoes

8 scallions

1 hard-cooked egg (optional)

1 cup low-fat mayonnaise

1 tsp paprika

salt and pepper

TO GARNISH

2 tbsp chopped fresh chives

pinch of paprika

COOK'S TIP

To make a lighter dressing, use
a mixture of half mayonnaise
and half plain yogurt.

1 Bring a large pan of lightly salted water to a boil. Add the potatoes to the pan and cook for about 10–15 minutes, or until they are just tender.

2 Drain the potatoes in a colander and rinse them under cold running water until they are completely cold. Drain them again thoroughly. Transfer the potatoes to a mixing bowl and set aside until required.

3 Trim and slice the scallions thinly on the diagonal. Chop the hard-cooked egg, if using.

4 Combine the mayonnaise, paprika, and salt and pepper to taste in a bowl until well blended. Pour the mixture over the potatoes.

5 Add the sliced scallions and chopped egg, if using, to the potatoes and toss together.

6 Transfer the potato salad to a serving bowl. Sprinkle with chopped chives and a pinch of paprika. Cover and chill in the refrigerator until ready to serve.

radish & cucumber salad

serves four

1 lb 2 oz/500 g new potatoes,
    scrubbed and halved

½ cucumber, sliced thinly

2 tsp salt

1 bunch of radishes, sliced thinly

DRESSING

1 tbsp Dijon mustard

2 tbsp olive oil

1 tbsp white wine vinegar

2 tbsp chopped mixed herbs

1 Cook the potatoes in a pan of boiling water for 10–15 minutes, or until tender. Drain thoroughly and set aside to cool.

2 Meanwhile, spread out the cucumber slices on a plate and sprinkle with the salt. Leave to stand for 30 minutes, then rinse under cold running water, and pat thoroughly dry with paper towels.

3 Arrange the cucumber and radish slices on a serving plate in a decorative pattern and pile the cooked potatoes in the center of the slices.

4 In a small bowl, combine all the dressing ingredients, whisking until thoroughly mixed. Pour the dressing over the salad, tossing well to coat all of the ingredients. Chill in the refrigerator before serving.

COOK'S TIP

The cucumber adds not only color but also a real freshness to the salad. It is salted and left to stand to remove the excess water, which would make the salad soggy. Wash the cucumber well to remove all of the salt before adding to the salad.

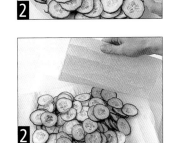

tuna niçoise salad

serves four

4 eggs

1 lb/450 g new potatoes

1 cup green beans, trimmed and
  halved

2 x 6 oz/175 g tuna steaks

6 tbsp olive oil, plus extra
  for brushing

1 garlic clove, crushed

1½ tsp Dijon mustard

2 tsp lemon juice

2 tbsp chopped fresh basil

2 Boston lettuces

1½ cups cherry tomatoes, halved

2 cups cucumber, peeled, halved,
  and sliced

½ cup pitted black olives

1¾ oz/50 g canned anchovies in
  oil, drained

salt and pepper

1 Bring a small pan of water to a boil. Add the eggs and then cook for 7–9 minutes from when the water returns to a boil: 7 minutes for a slightly soft center, 9 minutes for a firm center. Drain and refresh under cold running water. Set aside.

2 Cook the potatoes in boiling salted water for 10–12 minutes, until tender. Add the beans 3 minutes before the end of the cooking time. Drain both vegetables well and refresh under cold water. Drain well.

3 Wash and dry the tuna steaks. Brush with a little olive oil and season. Cook on a preheated ridged griddle pan for 2–3 minutes each side, until just tender but still slightly pink in the center. Set aside to rest.

4 Whisk together the garlic, mustard, lemon juice, basil, and seasoning. Whisk in the olive oil.

5 To assemble the salad, break apart the lettuces and tear into large pieces. Divide among individual serving plates. Next add the potatoes and beans, tomatoes, cucumber, and olives. Toss lightly together. Shell the eggs and quarter lengthwise. Arrange these on top of the salad. Sprinkle over the anchovies.

6 Flake the tuna steaks and arrange on the salads. Pour over the dressing and serve.

mixed vegetable salad

serves four

1 lb/450 g waxy new
  potatoes, scrubbed

1 carrot, cut into thin sticks

8 oz/225 g cauliflower flowerets

8 oz/225 g baby corn cobs,
  halved lengthwise

6 oz/175 g green beans

1 cup diced ham

1¾ oz/50 g mushrooms, sliced

salt and pepper

DRESSING

2 tbsp chopped fresh parsley

⅔ cup mayonnaise

⅔ cup plain yogurt

4 tsp lemon juice

grated rind of 1 lemon

2 tsp fennel seeds

1 Cook the potatoes in a large pan of boiling water for 15 minutes, or until tender. Drain thoroughly and let cool. When the potatoes are cold, slice them thinly.

2 Meanwhile, cook the carrot sticks, cauliflower flowerets, baby corn cobs, and green beans in a pan of boiling water for 5 minutes. Drain well and let cool.

COOK'S TIP

For a really quick salad, use a packet of frozen mixed vegetables, thawed, instead of fresh vegetables.

3 Reserving 1 teaspoon of the chopped parsley for the garnish, combine the remaining dressing ingredients in a bowl.

4 Arrange the vegetables on a salad platter and top with the diced ham and sliced mushrooms.

5 Spoon the dressing over the the salad and garnish with the reserved parsley. Serve immediately.

lobster salad & lime dressing

serves four

1 lb/450 g waxy potatoes, scrubbed
   and sliced

8 oz/225 g cooked lobster meat

⅔ cup mayonnaise

2 tbsp lime juice

finely grated rind of 1 lime

1 tbsp chopped fresh parsley

2 tbsp olive oil

2 tomatoes, seeded and diced

2 hard-cooked eggs, quartered

1 tbsp pitted green olives,
   quartered

salt and pepper

COOK'S TIP

As shellfish is used in this salad,
serve it immediately, or keep
covered and chilled for up to
1 hour before serving.

1 Cook the potatoes in a pan of boiling water for 10–15 minutes, or until cooked through. Drain well and set aside until required.

2 Remove the lobster meat from the shell and then separate it into large pieces.

3 In a medium bowl, combine the mayonnaise, 1 tbsp of the lime juice, half the grated lime rind, and half the chopped parsley, then set aside.

4 In a separate bowl, whisk the remaining lime juice with the olive oil and pour the dressing over the potatoes. Arrange the potatoes on a serving plate.

5 Top with the lobster meat, tomatoes, eggs, and olives. Season with salt and pepper and sprinkle with the reserved parsley.

6 Spoon the mayonnaise onto the center of the salad. Top with the reserved rind and serve.

spicy chicken salad

serves four

2 skinless, boneless chicken breast
    portions, about 4½ oz/125 g
    each

2 tbsp butter

1 fresh red chile, seeded
    and chopped

1 tbsp honey

½ tsp ground cumin

2 tbsp chopped fresh cilantro

3½ cups diced potatoes

1¾ oz/50 g green beans, halved

1 red bell pepper, seeded and cut
    into thin strips

2 tomatoes, seeded and diced

DRESSING

2 tbsp olive oil

pinch of chili powder

1 tbsp garlic wine vinegar

pinch of superfine sugar

1 tbsp chopped fresh cilantro

1 Cut the chicken into thin strips. Melt the butter in a heavy pan and add the chicken strips, fresh red chile, honey, and cumin. Cook for 10 minutes, turning until cooked through.

2 Transfer the mixture to a bowl and let cool, then stir in the chopped cilantro.

3 Meanwhile, cook the diced potatoes in a pan of boiling water for 10 minutes, until they are tender. Drain and let cool.

VARIATION

If you like, use lean turkey meat
instead of the chicken for
a slightly stronger taste. Use
the white meat for the best
appearance and flavor.

4 Blanch the green beans in a pan of boiling water for 3 minutes. Drain well and leave to cool. Combine the green beans and potatoes in a mixing bowl.

5 Add the bell pepper strips and tomatoes to the potato mixture. Stir in the chicken mixture.

6 In a small bowl, whisk the dressing ingredients together and pour the dressing over the salad, tossing well. Transfer the spicy chicken salad to a serving bowl or large platter and serve immediately.

indonesian chicken salad

serves four

2 lb 12 oz/1.25 kg waxy potatoes

10½ oz/300 g fresh pineapple,
   peeled and diced

2 carrots, grated

1¾ cups bean sprouts

1 bunch of scallions, sliced

1 large zucchini, cut into thin sticks

3 celery stalks, cut into thin sticks

6 oz/176 g unsalted peanuts

2 cooked skinless, boneless chicken
   breast portions, about 4½ oz/
   125 g each, sliced

DRESSING

6 tbsp crunchy peanut butter

6 tbsp olive oil

2 tbsp light soy sauce

1 fresh red chile, seeded
   and chopped

2 tsp sesame oil

4 tsp lime juice

1 Using a sharp knife, cut the potatoes into small dice. Bring a pan of water to the boil.

2 Cook the diced potatoes in the pan for about 10 minutes, or until tender. Drain them thoroughly in a colander and let cool until required.

3 Transfer the cooled potatoes to a salad bowl.

4 Add the diced pineapple, grated carrots, bean sprouts, scallions, zucchini and celery sticks, peanuts, and sliced chicken to the bowl of potatoes. Toss thoroughly to mix all the salad ingredients together.

5 To make the dressing, put the peanut butter in a small mixing bowl and gradually whisk in the olive oil and light soy sauce with a fork or a balloon whisk.

6 Stir in the chopped red chile, sesame oil, and lime juice. Mix well until combined.

7 Pour the spicy dressing over the salad and toss lightly to coat all of the ingredients. Serve the potato and chicken salad immediately.

italian sausage salad

serves four

1 lb/450 g waxy potatoes

1 radicchio or lollo rosso lettuce

1 green bell pepper, seeded
    and sliced

6 oz/175 g Italian sausage, sliced

1 red onion, halved and sliced

4½ oz/125 g sun-dried tomatoes in
    oil, drained and sliced

2 tbsp shredded fresh basil

DRESSING

1 tbsp balsamic vinegar

1 tsp tomato paste

2 tbsp olive oil

salt and pepper

1 Cook the potatoes in a large pan of boiling water for about 20 minutes, or until cooked through. Drain and let cool.

2 Separate the radicchio leaves or lollo rosso lettuce leaves. Line a large serving platter with the leaves.

3 Slice the cooled potatoes and arrange them in layers on the leaf-lined serving platter together with the sliced green bell pepper, sliced Italian sausage, red onion, and sun-dried tomatoes. Sprinkle with the shredded fresh basil.

4 In a small bowl, whisk the balsamic vinegar, tomato paste, and olive oil together and season to taste with salt and pepper. Pour the dressing over the potato salad and serve immediately.

COOK'S TIP

Any sliced Italian sausage or salami can be used in this salad.

potato, arugula, & apple salad

serves four

1 lb 5 oz/600 g potatoes, unpeeled
   and sliced

2 green eating apples, cored
   and diced

1 tsp lemon juice

¼ cup walnut pieces

4½ oz/125 g goat cheese, diced

5½ oz/150 g arugula leaves

salt and pepper

DRESSING

2 tbsp olive oil

1 tbsp red wine vinegar

1 tsp honey

1 tsp fennel seeds

COOK'S TIP

Serve this salad immediately it is ready to prevent the apple from turning an unappetizing brown color. Alternatively, prepare all of the other ingredients in advance, then core, dice, and add the apple at the last minute before serving.

1 Cook the potatoes in a pan of boiling water for 15 minutes, until tender. Drain thoroughly and let cool. Transfer the cooled potatoes to a serving bowl.

2 Toss the diced apples in the lemon juice, then drain, and stir them into the cold potatoes.

3 Add the walnut pieces, cheese cubes, and arugula leaves, then toss the salad to mix. Season to taste.

4 In a small bowl or pitcher, whisk the dressing ingredients together and then pour the dressing over the salad. Serve the potato, arugula, and apple salad immediately.

spicy sweet potato slices

serves four

1 lb/450 g sweet
   potatoes, unpeeled
2 tbsp sunflower oil
1 tsp chili sauce
salt and pepper

COOK'S TIP

For a simple spicy dip,
combine ⅔ cup sour cream
with ½ teaspoon sugar,
½ teaspoon Dijon mustard, and
salt and pepper to taste. Cover
with plastic wrap and chill in the
refrigerator until required.

1 Bring a large pan of water to a
boil. Add the sweet potatoes and
parboil them for 10 minutes, until
tender. Drain thoroughly and transfer
to a cutting board.

2 Peel the potatoes and cut them
into thick slices.

3 Combine the sunflower oil and
chili sauce in a small bowl.
Season to taste with salt and pepper
and mix well.

4 Brush the spicy mixture liberally
over one side of the potatoes.
Place the potatoes, oil side down, over
medium hot coals on a barbecue and
broil for 5–6 minutes.

5 Lightly brush the tops of the
potatoes with the oil, then turn
them over and broil for 5 minutes
more, or until crisp and golden.

6 Transfer the potatoes to a warm
serving dish and serve.

potato kibbeh

serves four

6 oz/175 g bulgur wheat

2 cups diced mealy potatoes

2 medium eggs

2 tbsp butter, melted

pinch of ground cumin

pinch of ground coriander

pinch of grated nutmeg

salt and pepper

vegetable oil, for deep-frying

parsley sprigs to garnish

salad to serve

STUFFING

6 oz/175 g ground lamb

1 small onion, chopped

1 tbsp pine nuts

1 oz/25 g dried apricots, chopped

pinch of grated nutmeg

pinch of ground cinnamon

1 tbsp chopped fresh cilantro

2 tbsp lamb stock

1 Put the bulgur wheat in a bowl and cover with boiling water. Soak for 30 minutes, until the water has been absorbed and the bulgur wheat has swollen.

2 Meanwhile, cook the diced potatoes in a pan of boiling water for 10 minutes, or until cooked through. Drain and mash until smooth.

3 Add the bulgur wheat to the mashed potato with the eggs, the melted butter, the ground cumin, and coriander, and the grated nutmeg. Mix well and season with salt and pepper.

4 To make the stuffing, dry-fry the lamb for 5 minutes. Add the onion and cook for 2–3 minutes more. Add the remaining stuffing

ingredients and cook for 5 minutes, until the lamb stock has been absorbed. Let the mixture cool slightly, then divide into 8 portions. Roll each portion into a ball.

5 Divide the potato mixture into 8 portions and flatten each into a circle. Place a portion of stuffing in the center of each circle. Shape the coating around the stuffing to encase it completely.

6 In a large pan or deep-fat fryer, heat the oil to 350–375°F/ 180–190°C or until a cube of bread browns in 30 seconds, and cook the kibbeh, in batches if necessary, for 5–7 minutes until golden brown. Drain well on paper towels, garnish, and serve the potato kibbeh with the salad.

potato & spinach triangles

serves four

2 tbsp butter, melted, plus extra
for greasing

1½ cups finely diced
waxy potatoes

1 lb 2 oz/500 g baby spinach

1 tomato, seeded and chopped

¼ tsp chili powder

½ tsp lemon juice

8 oz/225 g phyllo pastry, thawed
if frozen

salt and pepper

crisp salad, to serve

LEMON MAYONNAISE

⅔ cup mayonnaise

2 tsp lemon juice

grated rind of 1 lemon

COOK'S TIP

Buy unwaxed lemons for grating
or scrub well first.

1 Lightly grease a cookie sheet with a little butter.

2 Cook the potatoes in a pan of lightly salted, boiling water for 10 minutes, or until cooked through. Drain thoroughly and place in a mixing bowl.

3 Meanwhile, put the spinach in a pan with 2 tablespoonfuls of water. Cover and cook over low heat for 2 minutes, until wilted. Drain the spinach thoroughly, squeezing out excess moisture, and add to the potatoes.

4 Stir in the chopped tomato, chili powder, and lemon juice. Season to taste with salt and pepper.

5 Lightly brush 8 sheets of phyllo pastry with melted butter. Spread out 4 of the sheets and lay the other 4 on top of each. Using a sharp knife, cut them into rectangles about 8 x 4-inch/20 x 10-cm.

6 Spoon a little of the potato and spinach mixture onto one end of a pastry rectangle. Fold a corner of the pastry over the filling, fold the pointed end back over the pastry strip, then fold over the remaining pastry to form a triangle. Repeat with the remaining filling and pastry rectangles.

7 Place the triangles on the cookie sheet and bake in a preheated oven, 375°F/190°C for 20 minutes, or until golden brown.

8 To make the lemon mayonnaise, combine the mayonnaise, lemon juice, and lemon rind in a small bowl. Serve the potato and spinach triangles warm or cold with the bowl of lemon mayonnaise and a crisp salad.

curry pasties

serves four

2 cups all-purpose whole-wheat flour

⅓ cup margarine, cut into
small pieces

4 tbsp water

2 tbsp oil

8 oz/225 g diced root vegetables,
such as potatoes, carrots,
and parsnips

1 small onion, chopped

2 garlic cloves, finely chopped

½ tsp curry powder

½ tsp ground turmeric

½ tsp ground cumin

½ tsp whole-grain mustard

5 tbsp vegetable stock

soy milk, to glaze

1 Place the flour in a mixing bowl
and rub in the margarine with
your fingertips until the mixture
resembles bread crumbs. Stir in the
water and bring together to form a
soft dough. Wrap and chill in the
refrigerator for 30 minutes.

2 To make the filling, heat the oil in
a large pan. Add the diced root
vegetables, chopped onion, and garlic
and cook, stirring occasionally, for

2 minutes. Stir in all of the spices and
the mustard, turning the vegetables
to coat them thoroughly. Cook the
vegetables, stirring constantly, for
another minute.

3 Add the stock to the pan
and bring to a boil. Cover and
simmer, stirring occasionally, for about
20 minutes, until the vegetables are
tender and the liquid has been
absorbed. Let cool.

4 Divide the dough into 4 portions.
Roll each portion into a 6-inch/
15-cm circle. Place the filling on one
half of each circle.

5 Brush the edges of each circle
with soy milk, then fold over, and
press the edges firmly together to seal.
Place on a cookie sheet. Bake in a
preheated oven, 400°F/200°C, for
25–30 minutes, until golden brown.

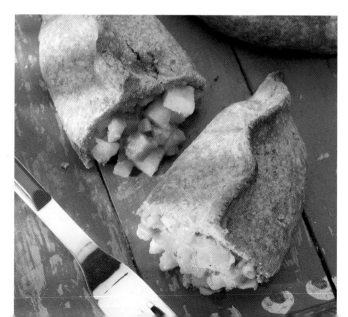

vegetable samosas

makes twelve

FILLING

2 tbsp vegetable oil

1 onion, chopped

½ tsp ground coriander

½ tsp ground cumin

pinch of ground turmeric

½ tsp ground ginger

½ tsp garam masala

1 garlic clove, crushed

1½ cups diced potatoes

1 cup frozen peas, thawed

5½ oz/150 g spinach, chopped

lemon wedges, to garnish

PASTRY

12 oz/350 g phyllo pastry

vegetable oil, for deep-frying

1 To make the filling, heat the oil in a skillet. Add the onion and sauté, stirring frequently, for 1–2 minutes, until softened. Stir in all of the spices and garlic and cook for 1 minute.

2 Add the potatoes and cook over low heat, stirring frequently, for 5 minutes, until they begin to soften.

3 Stir in the peas and spinach and cook for 3–4 minutes more.

4 Lay the phyllo pastry sheets out on a clean counter and fold 12 sheets in half lengthwise.

5 Place 2 tablespoons of the vegetable filling at one end of a folded pastry sheet. Fold over one corner to make a triangle. Continue folding in this way to make a triangular package and the seal the edges securely with water.

6 Repeat with the remaining pastry and the remaining filling.

7 Heat the oil for deep-frying to 350–375°F/180–190°C or until a cube of bread browns in 30 seconds. Fry the samosas, in batches, for 1–2 minutes until golden. Drain on absorbent paper towels and keep warm while you are cooking the remainder. Garnish and serve.

creamy stuffed mushrooms

serves four

1 oz/25 g dried ceps

1½ cups diced mealy potatoes

2 tbsp butter, melted

4 tbsp heavy cream

2 tbsp chopped fresh chives

8 large open-cup mushrooms

¼ cup grated Emmenthal cheese

⅔ cup vegetable stock

salt and pepper

fresh chives, to garnish

VARIATION

Use fresh mushrooms instead of the dried ceps, if you like, and stir a mixture of chopped nuts into the mushroom stuffing mixture for extra crunch.

1 Place the dried ceps in a small bowl. Add sufficient boiling water to cover and let soak for 20 minutes.

2 Meanwhile, cook the potatoes in a medium pan of lightly salted, boiling water for 10 minutes, until cooked through and tender. Drain well and mash until smooth with a fork or potato masher.

3 Drain the soaked ceps and then chop them finely. Mix them into the mashed potato.

4 Thoroughly blend the butter, cream, and chopped chives together and pour the mixture into the ceps and potato mixture, mixing well. Season to taste with salt and pepper.

5 Remove the stems from the open-cup mushrooms. Chop the stems and stir them into the potato mixture. Spoon the mixture into the open-cup mushrooms and sprinkle the cheese over the top.

6 Arrange the filled mushrooms in a shallow ovenproof dish and pour in the vegetable stock.

7 Cover the dish and cook in a preheated oven, 425°F/220°C, for 20 minutes. Remove the lid and cook for 5 minutes, until golden. Serve the mushrooms immediately, garnished with the fresh chives.

vegetable-stuffed parathas

serves six

DOUGH

1¾ cups whole-wheat flour
(ata or chapati flour), plus extra
for dusting

½ tsp salt

scant 1 cup water

about 4 tbsp vegetable ghee

FILLING

1 lb 8 oz/675 g potatoes

½ tsp ground turmeric

1 tsp garam masala

1 tsp finely chopped fresh
gingerroot

1 tbsp chopped fresh cilantro leaves

3 fresh green chiles, seeded and
finely chopped

1 tsp salt

1 To make the parathas, combine
the flour, salt, water, and
1¼ teaspoons of the ghee in a bowl to
form a dough.

2 Divide the dough into 6 equal
portions. Roll each portion out on
a floured counter. Brush the middle of
each of the dough portions with
½ teaspoon of the remaining ghee.
Fold the dough portions in half and roll
into a pipelike shape, then flatten with
the palms of your hands, and roll
around a finger to form a coil. Roll
out again, using flour to dust when
necessary, to form a circle about
7 inch/18 cm in diameter.

3 To make the filling, place the
potatoes in a large pan of boiling
water and cook until soft enough to
be mashed.

4 Blend the turmeric, garam
masala, ginger, cilantro leaves,
chiles, and salt together in a bowl.

5 Add the spice mixture to the
mashed potato and mix well.
Spread about 1 tablespoon of the spicy
potato mixture on each dough portion
and cover with another rolled-out piece
of dough. Seal the edges well.

6 Heat 2 teaspoons of the
remaining ghee in a heavy skillet.
Place the parathas gently in the skillet,
in batches, and cook, turning and
moving them about gently with a flat
spoon, until golden.

7 Remove the parathas from the
skillet and serve immediately,
while still warm.

COOK'S TIP

Clarified butter, known as ghee,
was once the main cooking fat in
India and Pakistan. It has largely
been superseded by vegetable
ghee, usually corn oil.

smoked fish & potato pâté

serves four

3⅔ cups diced mealy potatoes,

10½ oz/300 g smoked mackerel
fillets, skinned and flaked

2¾ oz/75 g cooked gooseberries

2 tsp lemon juice

2 tbsp sour cream

1 tbsp capers

1 gherkin, chopped

1 tbsp chopped dill pickle

1 tbsp chopped fresh dill

salt and pepper

lemon wedges, to garnish

toast or warm crusty bread, to serve

1 Cook the diced potatoes in a pan of boiling water for 10 minutes, until tender, then drain well.

2 Place the cooked potatoes in a food processor or blender.

3 Add the skinned and flaked smoked mackerel and process for 30 seconds, until fairly smooth. Alternatively, place the ingredients in a bowl and mash together with a fork.

4 Add the cooked gooseberries, lemon juice, and sour cream to the fish and potato mixture. Blend for another 10 seconds or mash well.

5 Stir in the capers, chopped gherkin, dill pickle, and chopped fresh dill. Season well with salt and pepper.

6 Turn the fish pâté into a serving dish. Garnish with lemon wedges and serve with slices of toast or warm crusty bread cut into chunks or slices.

COOK'S TIP

Use stewed, canned, or bottled cooked gooseberries for convenience and to save time, or when fresh gooseberries are out of season.

potato & pepperoni pizza

serves four

1 tbsp butter, plus extra for greasing

all-purpose flour, for dusting

generous 5 cups diced mealy potatoes

2 garlic cloves, crushed

2 tbsp chopped mixed fresh herbs

1 egg, beaten

6 tbsp bottled strained tomatoes

2 tbsp tomato paste

1¾ oz/50 g pepperoni slices

1 green bell pepper, seeded and cut
   into strips

1 yellow bell pepper, seeded and
   cut into strips

2 large open-cup mushrooms, sliced

¼ cup pitted black olives, cut
   into fourths

4½ oz/125 g mozzarella cheese,
   sliced

1 Grease and flour a 9-inch/23-cm pizza pan. Cook the potatoes in a pan of boiling water for 10 minutes, or until cooked through. Drain and mash until smooth. Transfer to a bowl and stir in the butter, garlic, herbs, and egg.

2 Spread the mixture into the prepared pizza pan. Cook in a preheated oven, 425°F/220°C, for

7–10 minutes, or until the pizza base begins to set.

3 Combine the bottled strained tomatoes and tomato paste and spoon it over the pizza base, to within ½-inch/1-cm of the edge of the base.

4 Arrange the pepperoni, bell peppers, mushrooms, and olives on top of the tomatoes.

5 Sprinkle the mozzarella cheese on top of the pizza. Return to the oven for 20 minutes, or until the base is cooked through and the cheese has melted on top. Serve hot.

potato & tomato calzone

serves four

DOUGH

4 cups strong white bread flour,
    plus extra for dusting

1 tsp active dry yeast

1¼ cups vegetable stock

1 tbsp honey

1 tsp caraway seeds

vegetable oil,
    for greasing

skim milk, for glazing

FILLING

1 tbsp vegetable oil

1⅓ cups diced waxy potatoes

1 onion, halved and sliced

2 garlic cloves, crushed

1½ oz/40 g sun-dried tomatoes

2 tbsp chopped fresh basil

2 tbsp tomato paste

2 celery stalks, sliced

½ cup grated mozzarella cheese

COOK'S TIP

Mozzarella di buffala, made from
the milk of the water buffalo, has
the best flavor. In any case, avoid
supermarket packets of ready-
grated mozzarella.

1 To make the dough, sift the flour into a large mixing bowl and stir in the yeast. Make a well in the center of the mixture. Stir in the vegetable stock, honey, and caraway seeds, and gradually bring the mixture together to form a dough.

2 Turn the dough out onto a lightly floured counter and knead for 8 minutes, until smooth. Place in a lightly oiled mixing bowl, then cover, and leave to rise in a warm place for 1 hour, or until it has doubled in size.

3 Meanwhile, make the filling. Heat the oil in a skillet and add all the remaining ingredients except for the cheese. Cook, stirring frequently, for about 5 minutes.

4 Divide the risen dough into 4 pieces. On a lightly floured counter, roll them out to form 4 x 7-inch/18-cm circles. Spoon equal amounts of the filling onto one half of each circle. Sprinkle the cheese over the filling. Brush the edge of the dough with milk and fold the dough over to form 4 semicircles, pressing firmly to seal the edges.

5 Place on a nonstick cookie sheet and brush with milk. Cook in a preheated oven, 425°F/220°C, for 30 minutes until golden and risen. Serve immediately.

salt cod hash

serves four

1 oz/25 g sea salt

1 lb 10 oz/750 g cod fillet

4 eggs

3 tbsp olive oil, plus extra
   for drizzling

8 bacon strips, chopped

generous 4 cups diced potatoes

8 garlic cloves

8 thick slices good-quality
   white bread

2 plum tomatoes, skinned
   and chopped

2 tsp red wine vinegar

2 tbsp chopped fresh parsley, plus
   extra to garnish

salt and pepper

lemon wedges,
   to garnish

1 Sprinkle the sea salt over both sides of the cod fillet. Place in a shallow dish, cover with plastic wrap, and chill in the refrigerator for 48 hours. When ready to cook, remove the cod from the refrigerator and rinse well under cold running water. Place in a shallow dish and soak in cold water for 2 hours, then drain well.

2 Bring a large pan of water to a boil and add the fish. Remove the pan from the heat and set aside for 10 minutes.

3 Drain the fish on paper towels and flake the flesh. Set aside. Discard the soaking water.

4 Bring a small pan of water to a boil. Add the eggs, bring back to the boil, and simmer for 7–9 minutes from when the water returns to the boil: 7 minutes for a slightly soft center, 9 minutes for a firm center. Drain, then plunge the eggs into cold water. Shell the eggs and coarsely chop. Set aside.

5 Heat the oil in a large skillet and add the bacon. Cook over medium heat for 4–5 minutes, until crisp. Remove and drain on paper towels. Put the potatoes and garlic in the skillet and cook over medium heat for 8–10 minutes, until crisp and golden. Meanwhile, toast the bread on both sides. Drizzle the bread with olive oil and set aside.

6 Add the tomatoes, bacon, fish, vinegar, and egg to the potatoes and garlic. Cook for 2 minutes. Stir in the parsley and season. Put the toast onto serving plates, top with the hash, and garnish with parsley and lemon.

bell pepper & mushroom hash

serves four

1lb 8 oz/675 g potatoes, diced

1 tbsp olive oil

2 garlic cloves, crushed

1 green bell pepper, seeded
   and diced

1 yellow bell pepper, seeded
   and diced

3 tomatoes, diced

1 cup white mushrooms, halved

1 tbsp Worcestershire sauce

2 tbsp chopped basil

salt and pepper

fresh basil sprigs, to garnish

warm crusty bread,
   to serve

COOK'S TIP

Most brands of Worcestershire sauce contain anchovies, so if you are vegetarian, check the label to make sure you choose a vegetarian variety.

1 Cook the potatoes in a large pan of lightly salted, boiling water for 7–8 minutes. Drain thoroughly and let cool slightly.

2 Heat the olive oil in a large, heavy skillet. Add the potatoes and cook over medium heat, stirring constantly, for 8–10 minutes, until golden brown all over.

3 Add the garlic and bell peppers and cook, stirring frequently, for 2–3 minutes.

4 Stir in the tomatoes and mushrooms and cook, stirring frequently, for 5–6 minutes.

5 Stir in the Worcestershire sauce and basil and season to taste with salt and pepper. Transfer to a warm serving dish. Garnish with basil sprigs and serve with warm crusty bread.

hash browns & tomato sauce

serves four

1 lb 2 oz/500 g waxy potatoes

1 carrot, diced

1 celery stalk, diced

1 cup diced white mushrooms

1 onion, diced

2 garlic cloves, crushed

¼ cup frozen peas, thawed

⅔ cup freshly grated Parmesan
    cheese

4 tbsp vegetable oil

2 tbsp butter

salt and pepper

SAUCE

1¼ cups bottled strained tomatoes

2 tbsp chopped
    fresh cilantro

1 tbsp Worcestershire sauce

½ tsp chili powder

2 tsp brown sugar

2 tsp mustard

5 tbsp vegetable`stock

1 Cook the potatoes in a pan of lightly salted, boiling water for 10 minutes. Drain and let cool. Meanwhile, cook the carrot in lightly salted, boiling water for 5 minutes.

2 When the potatoes are cool enough to handle, grate them with a coarse grater.

3 Drain the carrot and add it to the grated potato, together with the celery, mushrooms, onion, garlic, peas, and cheese. Season to taste with salt and pepper.

4 Put all of the sauce ingredients in a small pan and bring to a boil. Reduce the heat to low and simmer for 15 minutes.

5 Divide the potato mixture into 8 portions of equal size and shape into flattened rectangles with your hands.

6 Heat the oil and butter in a skillet and cook the hash browns, in batches, over low heat for about 4–5 minutes on each side, until crisp and golden brown.

7 Transfer the hash browns to a serving plate and serve immediately with the tomato sauce.

VARIATION

For an extra spicy tomato sauce, add 1 seeded and finely chopped fresh green chile with the other ingredients in step 4.

potato & cauliflower fritters

serves four

1½ cups diced mealy potatoes

8 oz/225 g cauliflower flowerets

scant ½ cup freshly grated
 Parmesan cheese

1 egg

1 egg white, for coating

vegetable oil, for deep-frying

paprika, for dusting (optional)

salt and pepper

crispy bacon strips, chopped,
 to serve

1 Cook the potatoes in a pan of boiling water for 10 minutes, until cooked through. Drain well and mash with a fork or potato masher.

2 Meanwhile, cook the cauliflower flowerets in a separate pan of boiling water for 10 minutes.

3 Drain the cauliflower flowerets thoroughly and gently mix into the mashed potato. Stir in the grated Parmesan cheese and season to taste with salt and pepper.

4 Separate the whole egg and beat the yolk into the potato and cauliflower, mixing well.

5 Lightly whisk both the egg whites in a clean bowl, then carefully fold into the potato and cauliflower mixture.

6 Divide the potato mixture into 8 equal portions and shape them into circles.

7 Pour the oil in a skillet until half-full, then heat it until hot. Cook the fritters for 3–5 minutes, turning once halfway through cooking.

8 Dust the cooked fritters with a little paprika, if you like, and serve with the crispy chopped bacon.

fritters with garlic sauce

serves four

1 lb 2 oz/500 g waxy
 potatoes, diced
1¼ cups freshly grated
 Parmesan cheese
vegetable oil, for deep-frying
SAUCE
2 tbsp butter
1 onion, halved and sliced
2 garlic cloves, crushed
¼ cup all-purpose flour
1¼ cups milk
1 tbsp chopped fresh parsley
BATTER
½ cup all-purpose flour
1 medium egg
⅔ cup milk

1 To make the sauce, melt the butter in a pan and cook the sliced onion and garlic over low heat, stirring frequently, for 2–3 minutes. Add the flour and cook, stirring constantly, for 1 minute.

2 Remove the pan from the heat and gradually stir in the milk and parsley. Return the pan to the heat and bring to a boil stirring constantly, until smooth. Keep warm.

3 Meanwhile, cook the diced potatoes in a pan of boiling water for 5–10 minutes, until just firm. Do not overcook or they will fall apart.

4 Drain the potatoes and toss them in the Parmesan cheese. If the potatoes are still slightly wet, the cheese sticks to them and coats them well.

5 To make the batter, place the flour in a mixing bowl and gradually beat in the egg and milk until smooth. Dip the potato cubes into the batter to coat them.

6 In a large pan, heat the oil to 350–375°F/180–190°C or until a cube of bread browns in 30 seconds.

Add the fritters, in batches, and cook for 3–4 minutes, or until golden.

7 Remove the fritters with a slotted spoon and drain thoroughly. Transfer them to a warm serving bowl and serve immediately with a bowl of the warm garlic sauce.

croquettes with ham

serves four

2½ cups diced mealy potatoes

1½ cups milk

2 tbsp butter

4 scallions, chopped

¾ cup grated Cheddar cheese

¾ cup chopped smoked ham

1 celery stalk, diced

1 egg, beaten

½ cup all-purpose flour

vegetable oil, for deep-frying

salt and pepper

TO GARNISH

tomato and cucumber wedges

COATING

2 eggs, beaten

4½ oz/125 g fresh whole-wheat
    bread crumbs

SAUCE

2 tbsp butter

¼ cup all-purpose flour

⅔ cup milk

⅔ cup vegetable bouillon

¾ cup grated Cheddar cheese,

1 tsp Dijon mustard

1 tbsp chopped fresh cilantro

1 Place the potatoes in a pan with the milk and bring to a boil. Reduce to a simmer until the liquid has been absorbed and the potatoes are cooked through and tender.

2 Add the butter and mash the potatoes. Stir in the scallions, cheese, ham, celery, egg, and flour. Season and leave to cool.

3 To make the coating, whisk the eggs in a bowl. Put the bread crumbs in a separate bowl.

4 Shape the potato mixture into 8 balls. First dip them in the egg, then in the bread crumbs.

5 To make the sauce, melt the butter in a small pan. Add the flour and cook for 1 minute. Remove from the heat and stir in the milk, bouillon, cheese, mustard, and cilantro. Bring to a boil, stirring until thickened. Reduce the heat and keep the sauce warm, stirring occasionally.

6 In a deep-fat fryer, heat the oil to 180–190°C/350–375°F and fry the croquettes, in batches, for about 5 minutes, until golden. Drain well, garnish and serve with the sauce.

VARIATION

Substitute cooked smoked
chicken for the ham and Fontina
cheese for the Cheddar.

pakoras

serves four

6 tbsp gram flour

½ tsp salt

1 tsp chili powder

1 tsp baking powder

1½ tsp white cumin seeds

1 tsp pomegranate seeds

1¼ cups water

1 tbsp chopped finely fresh
   cilantro leaves

vegetables of your choice:
   cauliflower, cut into small
   flowerets, onions cut into rings,
   sliced potatoes, sliced eggplant
   or bell pepper strips

vegetable oil, for deep-frying

fresh cilantro sprigs, to garnish

1 Sift the gram flour into a large mixing bowl. Add the salt, chili powder, baking powder, cumin, and pomegranate seeds, and blend together well. Pour in the water and beat thoroughly to form a smooth batter.

2 Add the cilantro and mix. Set the batter aside.

3 Dip the prepared vegetables of your choice, a few at a time, into the batter, carefully shaking off any of the excess.

COOK'S TIP

When cooking pakoras, it is important to use oil at the correct temperature. If the oil is too hot, the outside of the food will burn, as will the spices, before the inside is cooked. If the oil is too cool, the food will be soaked with oil before the batter becomes crisp.

4 Heat enough oil to cover the pakoras in a deep, heavy pan to 350°F/180°C. Place the battered vegetables in the oil and cook, in batches, turning once. Repeat until all the batter has been used.

5 Transfer the battered vegetables to paper towels and drain thoroughly. Place in a warmed dish, garnish and serve immediately.

chicken & herb fritters

serves four

2 cups mashed potato, with butter
   added

1⅓ cups chopped, cooked chicken

⅔ cups cooked ham, chopped finely

1 tbsp mixed herbs

2 eggs, lightly beaten

1 tbsp milk

fresh brown bread crumbs, to coat

oil, for shallow frying

salt and pepper

sprig of fresh parsley, to garnish

salad greens, to serve

1 In a large bowl, blend the potato, chicken, ham, herbs, and one of the eggs, and season well.

2 Shape the mixture into small balls or flat pancakes.

3 Add a little milk to the second egg and mix together.

COOK'S TIP

A mixture of chopped fresh
tarragon and parsley makes a
fresh and flavorsome addition to
these tasty fritters.

4 Place the bread crumbs on a plate. Dip the balls in the egg and milk mixture, then roll in the bread crumbs to coat them completely.

5 Heat the oil in a large skillet and cook the fritters, turning once, until they are golden brown on both sides. Garnish with a sprig of fresh parsley and serve at once with fresh salad greens.

vegetable kabobs

makes twelve

3½ cups potatoes, sliced

1 onion, sliced

½ medium cauliflower, cut into
small flowerets

scant ½ cup peas

1 tbsp spinach paste

2–3 fresh green chiles

1 tbsp fresh cilantro leaves

1 tsp finely chopped fresh
gingerroot

1 tsp crushed garlic

1 tsp ground coriander

pinch of ground turmeric

1 tsp salt

1 cup bread crumbs

1¼ cups vegetable oil

fresh chile strips, to garnish

1 Place the potatoes, onion, and cauliflower flowerets in a large pan of water and bring to a boil. Reduce the heat and simmer gently until the potatoes are cooked through. Remove the vegetables from the pan with a slotted spoon, drain thoroughly and transfer to a bowl.

2 Add the peas and spinach paste to the vegetables and mix well, mashing down thoroughly with a fork or wooden spoon.

3 Using a sharp knife, finely chop the green chiles and fresh cilantro leaves.

4 Mix the chiles and cilantro leaves with the ginger, garlic, ground coriander, turmeric, and salt.

5 Blend the spice mixture into the vegetables, mixing with a fork to make a paste.

6 Spread out the bread crumbs on a large plate.

7 Break off 10–12 small balls from the spice paste. Flatten them with the palm of your hand to make flat, round shapes.

8 Dip each kabob in the bread crumbs, coating well.

9 Heat the oil in a heavy skillet and cook the kabobs, in batches, until golden brown, turning occasionally. Transfer to warm serving plates and garnish with fresh chile strips. Serve immediately, while still hot.

cheese & onion röstis

serves four

2 lb/900 g potatoes

1 onion, grated

½ cup grated Gruyère cheese

2 tbsp chopped fresh parsley

1 tbsp olive oil

2 tbsp butter

salt and pepper

TO GARNISH

1 shredded scallion

1 small tomato, cut into wedges

1 Parboil the potatoes in a pan of lightly salted, boiling water for 10 minutes and let cool. Peel the potatoes and grate with a coarse grater. Place the grated potatoes in a large mixing bowl.

2 Stir in the onion, cheese, and parsley. Season well with salt and pepper. Divide the potato mixture into 4 portions of equal size and form them into cakes.

3 Heat half of the olive oil with half of the butter in a skillet. Cook 2 of the potato cakes over high heat for 1 minute, then reduce the heat and cook for 5 minutes, until they are golden underneath. Turn them over and cook for 5 minutes more.

4 Repeat with the other half of the oil and the remaining butter to cook the remaining 2 cakes. Transfer to warm individual serving plates. Garnish with the shredded scallions and tomato wedges and serve immediately.

COOK'S TIP

The potato cakes should be flattened as much as possible during cooking, otherwise the outsides will be cooked before the centers.

sweet potato cakes

serves four

1 lb 2 oz/500 g sweet potatoes

2 garlic cloves, crushed

1 small fresh green chile, seeded
   and chopped

2 fresh cilantro sprigs, chopped

1 tbsp dark soy sauce

all-purpose flour, for shaping

vegetable oil, for frying

sesame seeds, for sprinkling

SOY-TOMATO SAUCE

2 tsp vegetable oil

1 garlic clove, chopped finely

1½ tsp finely chopped fresh
   gingerroot

3 tomatoes, skinned and chopped

2 tbsp dark soy sauce

1 tbsp lime juice

2 tbsp chopped fresh cilantro

1 To make the soy-tomato sauce, heat the oil in a wok and stir-fry the garlic and ginger over medium heat for about 1 minute. Add the tomatoes and stir-fry for 2 minutes more. Remove the wok from the heat and stir in the soy sauce, lime juice, and chopped cilantro. Set aside and keep warm.

2 Peel the sweet potatoes and grate finely (you can do this quickly with a food processor). Place the garlic, chile, and cilantro in a mortar and crush to a smooth paste with a pestle. Stir in the soy sauce mix with the sweet potatoes.

3 Divide the mixture into 12 equal portions. Dip into flour and pat into a flat, round patty shape.

4 Heat a shallow layer of oil in a wide skillet. Fry the sweet potato cakes, in batches, over high heat until golden, turning once.

5 Drain the potato cakes on paper towels and sprinkle with sesame seeds. Transfer to warm plates and serve with a spoonful of the soy-tomato sauce.

93

potato & spinach gnocchi

serves four

1⅔ cups diced mealy potatoes

6 oz/175 g spinach

1 egg yolk

1 tsp olive oil

1 cup all-purpose flour

salt and pepper

spinach leaves, to garnish

SAUCE

1 tbsp olive oil

2 shallots, chopped

1 garlic clove, crushed

1¼ cups bottled strained tomatoes

2 tsp soft light brown sugar

VARIATION

Add chopped fresh herbs and cheese to the gnocchi dough instead of the spinach, if you like.

1 Cook the diced potatoes in a pan of boiling water for 10 minutes, or until cooked through. Drain and mash the potatoes.

2 Meanwhile, in a separate pan, blanch the spinach in a little boiling water for 1–2 minutes. Drain the spinach and shred the leaves.

3 Transfer the mashed potato to a lightly floured cutting board and make a well in the center. Add the egg yolk, olive oil, spinach, and a little of the flour. Quickly mix the ingredients into the potato, adding more flour as you go, until you have a smooth, firm dough. Divide the mixture into very small dumplings.

4 Cook the gnocchi, in batches, in a pan of lightly salted, boiling water for about 5 minutes, or until they rise to the surface.

5 Meanwhile, make the sauce. Put the oil, shallots, garlic, bottled strained tomatoes, and sugar into a pan and cook over low heat for 10–15 minutes, or until the sauce has thickened and reduced.

6 Drain the gnocchi using a slotted spoon and transfer to warm serving dishes. Spoon the sauce over the gnocchi and garnish with the fresh spinach leaves.

vegetable cake

serves four

BASE

2 tbsp vegetable oil, plus extra
    for brushing

2lb 12 oz/1.25 kg large waxy
    potatoes, sliced thinly

TOPPING

1 tbsp vegetable oil

1 leek, chopped

1 zucchini, grated

1 red bell pepper, seeded and diced

1 green bell pepper, seeded and diced

1 carrot, grated

2 tsp chopped fresh parsley

1 cup soft cheese

¼ cup grated sharp cheese

2 eggs, beaten

salt and pepper

shredded cooked leek, to garnish

salad, to serve

1 Brush an 8-inch/20-cm loose bottomed cake pan with oil.

2 To make the base, heat the oil in a skillet. Cook the potato slices until softened and browned. Drain on paper towels and place in the base of the pan.

3 To make the topping, heat the oil in a separate large, heavy skillet. Add the leek and cook over low heat, stirring frequently, for 3–4 minutes, until softened but not colored.

4 Add the grated zucchini, diced bell peppers, grated carrot, and chopped parsley to the skillet and cook over low heat, stirring occasionally, for 5–7 minutes, or until the vegetables have softened.

5 Meanwhile, beat both types of cheese and the eggs together in a large bowl. Stir in the vegetables and season to taste with salt and pepper. Spoon the mixture evenly over the potato base.

6 Cook in a preheated oven, 375°F/190°C, for 20–25 minutes, until the cake is set.

7 Remove the vegetable cake from the pan and transfer to a warm serving plate. Garnish with shredded leek and serve with a crisp salad.

feta & spinach omelet

serves four

6 tbsp butter

8 cups diced waxy potatoes

3 garlic cloves, crushed

1 tsp paprika

2 tomatoes, skinned, seeded,
   and diced

12 eggs

pepper

FILLING

8 oz/225 g baby spinach

1 tsp fennel seeds

4½ oz/125 g feta cheese, diced

4 tbsp plain yogurt

1 Heat 2 tablespoons of the butter in a skillet and cook the potatoes over low heat, stirring constantly, for 7–10 minutes, until golden. Transfer to a bowl.

2 Add the garlic, paprika, and tomatoes to the skillet and cook for 2 minutes more.

3 Whisk the eggs together and season with pepper. Pour the eggs into the potatoes and mix well.

4 Cook the spinach in boiling water for 1 minute, until just wilted. Drain and refresh under cold running water. Pat dry with paper towels. Stir in the fennel seeds, feta cheese, and yogurt.

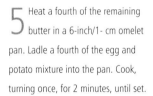

5 Heat a fourth of the remaining butter in a 6-inch/1- cm omelet pan. Ladle a fourth of the egg and potato mixture into the pan. Cook, turning once, for 2 minutes, until set.

6 Transfer the omelet to a serving plate. Spoon a fourth of the spinach mixture onto one half of the omelet, fold the omelet in half over the filling. Repeat to make a further 3 omelets, then serve.

baked potatoes with salsa

serves four

4 baking potatoes

1 large ripe avocado

1 tsp lemon juice

6 oz/175 g smoked bean
  curd, diced

2 garlic cloves, crushed

1 onion, chopped finely

1 tomato, chopped finely

4½ oz/125 g mixed salad greens

fresh cilantro sprigs, to garnish

SALSA

2 ripe tomatoes, seeded
  and diced

1 tbsp chopped fresh cilantro

1 shallot, finely diced

1 fresh green chile, seeded
  and diced

1 tbsp lemon or lime juice

salt and pepper

1 Scrub the potatoes and prick the skins with a fork. Rub a little salt into the skins and place them on a cookie sheet.

2 Cook in a preheated oven, 375°F/190°C, for 1 hour, or until cooked through and soft and the skins are crisp.

3 Cut the potatoes in half lengthwise and scoop the flesh into a bowl, leaving a thin layer of potato inside the shells.

4 Halve and pit the avocado. Using a spoon, scoop out the avocado flesh and add to the bowl containing the potato. Stir in the lemon or lime juice and mash the mixture together with a fork until fairly smooth. Mix in the bean curd, garlic, onion, and tomato. Spoon the mixture into one half of the potato shells.

5 Arrange the salad greens over the avocado mixture and place the other half of the potato shell on top.

6 To make the salsa, combine the tomatoes, cilantro, shallot, chile, lemon juice, and salt and pepper to taste. Garnish the potatoes with sprigs of fresh cilantro and serve with the salsa.

COOK'S TIP

Avocados vary in color from brownish-purple to green, the skin may be smooth or knobby, and the shape varies from small and relatively round to long and pear-shaped. Whatever variety you buy, test for ripeness by gently cupping the stalk end. It should just yield to pressure, but should not be soft or squashy. Use ripe avocados immediately.

baked pesto potatoes

serves four

4 baking potatoes

⅔ cup heavy cream

⅓ cup vegetable bouillon

1 tbsp lemon juice

2 garlic cloves, crushed

3 tbsp chopped basil

2 tbsp pine nuts

scant ½ cup freshly grated
Parmesan cheese

salt and pepper

1 Scrub the potatoes well and prick the skins with a fork. Rub a little salt into the skins and place on a cookie sheet.

2 Cook in a preheated oven, 375°F/190°C, for 1 hour, or until the potatoes are cooked through and the skins are crisp.

3 Remove the potatoes from the oven and cut them in half lengthwise. Using a spoon, scoop the potato flesh into a mixing bowl, leaving a thin shell of potato inside the skins. Mash the potato flesh with a fork or potato masher.

4 Meanwhile, mix the cream and bouillon in a pan and simmer over a low heat for about 8–10 minutes, or until reduced by half.

5 Stir in the lemon juice, garlic, and chopped basil, and season to taste with salt and pepper. Stir the mixture into the mashed potato flesh, together with the pine nuts.

6 Spoon the mixture back into the potato shells and sprinkle the Parmesan cheese on top. Return the potatoes to the oven for 10 minutes, or until the cheese has browned. Serve.

baked potatoes with beans

serves six

4 lb/1.8 kg potatoes

4 tbsp vegetable ghee or oil

1 large onion, chopped

2 garlic cloves, crushed

1 tsp ground turmeric

1 tbsp cumin seeds

2 tbsp mild or medium curry paste

12 oz/350 g cherry tomatoes

14 oz/400 g canned black-eye peas,
    drained and rinsed

14 oz/400 g canned red kidney
    beans, drained and rinsed

1 tbsp lemon juice

2 tbsp tomato paste

⅔ cup water

2 tbsp chopped fresh mint
    or cilantro

salt and pepper

1 Scrub the potatoes and prick several times with a fork. Place in a preheated oven, 350°F/180°C, and then cook for 1–1¼ hours, or until the potatoes feel soft when gently squeezed between finger and thumb.

2 About 20 minutes before the end of cooking time, prepare the topping. Heat the ghee or oil in a pan, then cook the onion over low heat, stirring frequently, for 5 minutes. Add the garlic, turmeric, cumin seeds, and curry paste and cook for 1 minute.

3 Stir in the tomatoes, black-eye peas, red kidney beans, lemon juice, tomato paste, water, and chopped mint. Season to taste with salt and pepper, then cover and simmer over low heat, stirring frequently, for 10 minutes.

4 When the potatoes are cooked, cut them in half and mash the flesh lightly with a fork. Spoon the prepared peas and beans mixture on top. Place on warmed serving plates and serve immediately.

sweet potato & leek patties

serves four

2 lb/900 g sweet potato

4 tsp sunflower oil

2 leeks, trimmed and chopped finely

1 garlic clove, crushed

2 tsp finely chopped fresh
   gingerroot

7 oz /200g canned corn
   kernels, drained

2 tbsp low-fat plain yogurt

generous ½ cup whole-wheat flour

salt and pepper

GINGER SAUCE

2 tbsp white wine vinegar

2 tsp superfine sugar

1 fresh red chile, seeded
   and chopped

1-inch/2.5-cm piece fresh
   gingerroot, cut into thin strips

2 tbsp ginger wine

4 tbsp vegetable bouillon

1 tsp cornstarch

TO SERVE

lettuce leaves

1 scallion, shredded

1 Peel the potatoes. Cut into thick cubes and cook in boiling water for 10–15 minutes. Drain well and mash. Let cool.

2 Heat 2 teaspoons of the oil and cook the leeks, garlic, and ginger for 2–3 minutes. Stir into the potato with the corn, yogurt, and seasoning. Form into 8 patties and toss in the flour. Chill for 30 minutes. Place the patties on a preheated broiler rack and lightly brush with the remaining oil. Broil for 5 minutes, then turn over, and broil for 5 minutes more.

3 Place the vinegar, sugar, chile, and ginger in a pan and simmer for 5 minutes. Stir in the wine. Blend the bouillon and cornstarch and add to the sauce, stirring, until thickened. Serve the patties with lettuce and scallions, and the sauce.

mixed mushroom cakes

serves four

2¾ cups diced mealy potatoes

2 tbsp butter

6 oz/175 g mixed
mushrooms, chopped

2 garlic cloves, crushed

1 medium egg, beaten

1 tbsp chopped fresh chives, plus
extra to garnish

all-purpose flour, for dusting

vegetable oil, for deep-frying

salt and pepper

salad, to serve

4 Stir the mushrooms and garlic into the potato, together with the beaten egg and chives.

5 Divide the mixture equally into 4 portions and shape them into round cakes. Toss them in the flour until the outsides of the cakes are completely coated.

6 Pour the oil into the skillet until it is half-full, then heat it until it is hot. Add the potato cakes and cook over medium heat for 10 minutes, until they are golden brown, turning them over halfway through. Serve the cakes immediately, with a simple crisp salad.

1 Cook the potatoes in a pan of lightly salted boiling water for 10 minutes, or until cooked through.

2 Drain the potatoes well. Mash with a potato masher or fork and set aside.

3 Meanwhile, melt the butter in a skillet. Add the mushrooms and garlic and cook, stirring constantly, for 5 minutes. Drain well.

shrimp röstis

serves four

12 oz/350 g potatoes

12 oz/350 g celery root

1 carrot

1 small onion

8 oz/225 g cooked shelled shrimp,
    thawed if frozen and well-
    drained on paper towels

¼ cup all-purpose flour

1 egg, lightly beaten

vegetable oil, for deep-frying

salt and pepper

salad leaves, to serve

CHERRY TOMATO SALSA

8 oz/225 g mixed cherry tomatoes
    such as baby plum, yellow and
    orange, quartered

1 small mango, finely diced

1 fresh red chile, seeded and
    chopped finely

1 small red onion, chopped finely

1 tbsp chopped cilantro

1 tbsp chopped fresh chives

2 tbsp olive oil

2 tsp lemon juice

salt and pepper

1 For the salsa, combine the tomatoes, mango, chile, red onion, cilantro, chives, olive oil, lemon juice, and seasoning. Set aside for the flavors to steep.

2 Using a food processor or the fine blade of a box grater, finely grate the potatoes, celery root, carrot, and onion. Combine the grated vegetables with the shrimp, flour, and egg. Season well and set aside.

3 Divide the shrimp mixture into 8 equal pieces. Press each into a greased 4-inch/10-cm cutter (if you have only 1 cutter, simply shape the röstis individually).

4 In a large skillet, heat a shallow layer of oil. When hot, transfer the shrimp cakes, still in the cutters, to the skillet, in 4 batches if necessary (preheat oven to keep them warm.) When the oil sizzles underneath, remove the cutter. Cook gently, pressing down with a metal spatula, for 6–8 minutes on each side, until browned and the vegetables are tender. Drain on paper towels and keep warm. Serve with the tomato salsa and salad.

salmon pancakes

serves four

2¼ cups grated mealy potatoes

2 scallions, chopped

2 tbsp self-rising flour

2 eggs, beaten

2 tbsp vegetable oil

salt and pepper

fresh chives, to garnish

TOPPING

⅔ cup sour cream

4½ oz/125 g smoked salmon

1 Rinse the grated potatoes under cold running water. Drain and pat dry on paper towels. Transfer to a mixing bowl.

2 Mix the chopped scallions, flour, and eggs into the potatoes and season well with salt and pepper.

3 Heat 1 tablespoon of the oil in a skillet. Drop about 4 tablespoonfuls of the mixture into the skillet and spread each one with the

back of a spoon to form a circle (the mixture should make 16 pancakes.) Cook for 5–7 minutes, turning once, until golden. Drain well.

4 Heat the remaining oil and cook the remaining mixture in batches.

5 Top the pancakes with the sour cream and smoked salmon. Garnish with fresh chives and serve hot.

tuna fishcakes

serves four

8 oz/225 g potatoes, diced

1 tbsp olive oil

1 large shallot, chopped finely

1 garlic clove, chopped finely

1 tsp fresh thyme leaves

14 oz/400 g canned tuna in olive oil, drained

grated rind ½ lemon

1 tbsp chopped fresh parsley

2–3 tbsp all-purpose flour

1 egg, lightly beaten

2 cups fresh bread crumbs

vegetable oil, for shallow frying

salt and pepper

salad to serve

QUICK TOMATO SAUCE

2 tbsp olive oil

14 oz/400 g canned chopped tomatoes

1 garlic clove, crushed

1 tsp sugar

grated rind 1 lemon

1 tbsp chopped fresh basil

1 For the tuna fishcakes, cook the potatoes in plenty of boiling salted water for 12–15 minutes, until tender. Mash, leaving a few lumps, and set aside.

2 Heat the oil in a small skillet and cook the shallot gently for 5 minutes, until softened. Add the garlic and thyme leaves and cook for 1 minute more. Let cool slightly, then add to the potatoes with the tuna, lemon rind, and parsley, Season to taste with salt and pepper. Mix together well, but leave some texture.

3 Form the mixture into 6–8 cakes. Dip the cakes first in the flour, then the egg, and, finally, the bread crumbs to coat. Chill in the refrigerator for 30 minutes.

4 Meanwhile, make the tomato sauce. Put all the ingredients into a pan and bring to a boil. Cover and simmer gently for 30 minutes. Uncover and simmer for 15 minutes more, until thickened and reduced.

5 Heat enough oil in a skillet to cover the base generously. When hot, add the chilled fishcakes, in batches, and cook for 3–4 minutes on each side, until golden and crisp. Drain on paper towels while you cook the remaining fishcakes. Serve hot with the tomato sauce and salad.

potato stir-fry

serves four

2lb/900 g waxy potatoes

2 tbsp vegetable oil

1 yellow bell pepper, seeded
    and diced

1 red bell pepper, seeded and diced

1 carrot, cut into thin strips

1 zucchini, cut into thin strips

2 garlic cloves, crushed

1 fresh red chile, seeded
    and sliced

1 bunch of scallions,
    halved lengthwise

½ cup coconut milk

1 tsp chopped lemongrass

2 tsp lime juice

finely grated rind of 1 lime

1 tbsp chopped fresh cilantro

COOK'S TIP

Make sure that you use a waxy
variety of potato that will keep
its shape when cooked. Check
that the potatoes are
not overcooked in step 2,
otherwise the potato pieces
will disintegrate when they
are stir-fried in the wok.

1 Using a sharp knife, cut the
potatoes into small dice.

2 Bring a large pan of water to a
boil, add the diced potatoes and
simmer gently for 5 minutes. Drain
thoroughly and set aside.

3 Heat a wok then add the
vegetable oil, swirling the oil
around the base of the wok until it is
really hot.

4 Add the potatoes, diced bell
peppers, carrot, zucchini, garlic,
and chile to the wok, and stir-fry the
vegetables for 2–3 minutes, until
tender but still crisp.

5 Stir in the scallions, coconut milk,
chopped lemongrass, and lime
juice, and stir-fry the mixture for about
5 minutes more.

6 Add the lime rind and chopped
cilantro and stir-fry for 1 minute.
Serve hot.

VARIATION

Before stir-frying the vegetables,
make an omelet garnish. Whisk
2 eggs with 2 tablespoons water,
3 tablespoons chopped fresh
cilantro, and seasoning. Heat
1 tablespoon of vegetable oil in
the wok and cook over high heat
until the edges are crisp. Flip
over and cook the second side
for 30 seconds. Slide the omelet
onto a board and leave to cool.
Roll up loosely and cut into
thin slices.

Side Dishes

When the potato is thought of as a component of a meal, it is inevitably associated with meat and vegetables, and is served either roasted or boiled. In fact, the potato is so versatile in its ability to combine with other flavorings and be cooked in so many different ways that it is the perfect base for a whole variety of delicious side dishes. This chapter demonstrates that versatility with a wide range of tantalizing recipes.

Potatoes can be cooked and served in many different ways, such as mashing, roasting, stir-frying, pan-frying, deep-frying, baking, and boiling. You will find all kinds of different recipes for side dishes in this chapter, including Spanish Potatoes and Potatoes en Papillotes. There are also classic recipes, such as Potatoes Dauphinois and Pommes Anna, as well as updated versions of traditional dishes, such as Chili Roast Potatoes and Spicy Potato Fries.

colcannon

serves four

8 oz/225 g green
  cabbage, shredded

5 tbsp milk

1½ cup diced mealy potatoes

1 large leek, chopped

pinch of freshly grated nutmeg

1 tbsp butter, melted

salt and pepper

COOK'S TIP

There are many different varieties
of cabbage, which produce
hearts at varying times of year,
so you can be sure of being able
to make this delicious cabbage
dish all year round.

1 Cook the shredded cabbage in a pan of boiling salted water for 7–10 minutes. Drain thoroughly and set aside.

2 Meanwhile, in a separate pan, bring the milk to a boil and add the potatoes and leek. Reduce the heat and simmer for 15–20 minutes, or until they are cooked through.

3 Stir in the grated nutmeg and thoroughly mash the potatoes and leek together with a fork or a potato masher.

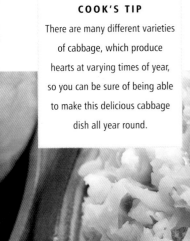

4 Add the drained cabbage to the mashed potato and leek mixture and mix well. Season to taste with salt and pepper.

5 Spoon the mixture into a warmed serving dish, making a shallow hollow in the center with the back of a tablespoon.

6 Carefully pour the melted butter into the hollow and serve the colcannon immediately.

spanish potatoes

serves four

2 tbsp olive oil

1 lb 2 oz/500 g small new
potatoes, halved

1 onion, halved and sliced

1 green bell pepper, seeded and cut
into strips

1 tsp chili powder

1 tsp prepared mustard

1¼ cups bottled strained tomatoes

1¼ cups vegetable bouillon

salt and pepper

chopped fresh parsley, to garnish

COOK'S TIP

In Spain, tapas are traditionally
served with a glass of chilled
sherry or some other aperitif.

1 Heat the olive oil in a large, heavy
skillet. Add the halved new
potatoes and the sliced onion and cook
over medium heat, stirring frequently,
for about 4–5 minutes, until the onion
slices are soft and translucent but
not colored.

2 Add the green bell pepper strips,
chili powder, and mustard to the
pan and cook for 2–3 minutes more.

3 Stir the bottled strained tomatoes
and the vegetable bouillon into
the pan and bring to a boil. Reduce the
heat and simmer for about 25 minutes,
or until the potatoes are tender.

4 Transfer the potatoes to a
warmed serving dish. Sprinkle the
parsley over the top and serve
immediately. Alternatively, leave the
Spanish potatoes to cool completely
and serve at room temperature.

cheese crumble-topped mash

serves four

generous 5 cups diced mealy potatoes

2 tbsp butter

2 tbsp milk

½ cup grated sharp cheese or
   blue cheese

CRUMBLY TOPPING

3 tbsp butter

1 onion, cut into chunks

1 garlic clove, crushed

1 tbsp whole-grain mustard

3 cups fresh whole-wheat
   bread crumbs

2 tbsp chopped fresh parsley

salt and pepper

VARIATION

Substitute plain yogurt for the
milk, and Parmesan for sharp
cheese. Alternatively, omit the
cheese and stir in 1¾ cups
chopped walnuts. Or substitute
young parsnips or celery root for
half the potatoes. For a richer
texture use heavy cream
instead of milk.

1 Cook the potatoes in a pan of boiling water for 10 minutes, or until they are cooked through.

2 Meanwhile, make the crumbly topping. Melt the butter in a skillet. Add the onion, garlic, and mustard and cook gently for 5 minutes, until the onion chunks have softened, stirring constantly.

3 Put the bread crumbs in a medium mixing bowl and stir in the fried onion mixture. Season to taste with salt and pepper.

4 Drain the potatoes thoroughly and place them in a mixing bowl. Add the butter and milk, then mash until smooth. Stir in the grated cheese while the potato is still hot.

5 Spoon the mashed potato into a shallow ovenproof dish and sprinkle with the crumbly topping.

6 Cook in a preheated oven, 400°F/200°C, for 10–15 minutes, until the crumbly topping is golden brown and crunchy. Serve immediately, straight from the dish.

COOK'S TIP

For extra crunch, add freshly
cooked vegetables, such as
celery and bell peppers, to the
mashed potato in step 4.

potatoes en papillotes

serves four

1 lb/450 g small new potatoes

1 carrot, cut into thin batons

1 fennel bulb, sliced

2¾ oz/75 g green beans

1 yellow bell pepper, seeded and
cut into strips

16 tbsp dry white wine

4 rosemary sprigs

salt and pepper

fresh rosemary sprigs, to garnish

1 Cut 4 squares of waxed paper
measuring about 10-inch/
25-cm in size.

2 Divide the vegetables equally
among the 4 paper squares,
placing them in the center.

3 Bring the edges of the paper
together and scrunch them
together to encase the vegetables,
leaving the top open.

4 Place the parcels in a shallow
roasting pan and spoon
4 tablespoons of white wine into each
parcel. Add a rosemary sprig and
season with salt and pepper.

5 Fold the top of each parcel over to
seal it securely. Cook them in a
preheated oven, 375°F/190°C, for
30–35 minutes, or until the vegetables
are tender.

6 Transfer the sealed parcels to
4 individual serving plates and
garnish with rosemary sprigs.

7 Open the parcels at the table for
the full aroma of the vegetables
to be appreciated.

gingered potatoes

serves four

1½ lb/675 g waxy potatoes, diced

2 tbsp vegetable oil

4 tsp grated fresh gingerroot

1 fresh green chile, seeded
and chopped

1 celery stalk, chopped

¼ cup cashew nuts

a few saffron threads

3 tbsp boiling water

5 tbsp butter

celery leaves, to garnish

COOK'S TIP

Use a nonstick, heavy skillet,
because the potato mixture is
fairly dry and is likely to stick to
an ordinary skillet.

1 Cook the diced potatoes in a
large pan of boiling water for
about 10 minutes, until just cooked
and tender, then tip into a colander,
and drain them thoroughly.

2 Heat the vegetable oil in a heavy
skillet and add the potatoes. Cook
over medium heat, stirring constantly,
for 3–4 minutes.

3 Add the grated ginger, green
chile, celery, and cashew nuts and
cook for 1 minute.

4 Meanwhile, place the saffron
threads in a small bowl. Add the
measured boiling water and let soak
for 5 minutes.

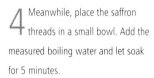

5 Add the butter to the skillet, then
lower the heat, and stir in the
saffron mixture. Cook over low heat for
about 10 minutes, or until the potatoes
are tender.

6 Transfer the mixture to a warm
serving dish. Garnish the
gingered potatoes with the celery
leaves and serve immediately.

trio of potato purées

serves four

1 tbsp butter, plus extra for greasing

10½ oz/300 g mealy
   potatoes, chopped

4½ oz/125 g rutabaga, chopped

1 carrot, chopped

1 lb/450 g fresh spinach

1 tbsp skim milk

¼ cup all-purpose flour

1 egg

½ tsp ground cinnamon

1 tbsp orange juice

¼ tsp grated nutmeg

salt and pepper

carrot batons, to garnish

1 Lightly grease 4 x ⅔ cup ramekins with butter.

2 Cook the potatoes in a pan of boiling water for 10 minutes. In separate pans cook the rutabaga and carrot in boiling water for 10 minutes. Blanch the spinach in boiling water for 5 minutes. Drain the vegetables.

3 Add the milk and the tablespoon of butter to the potatoes, mash until smooth with a fork or a potato masher. Stir in the flour and egg.

4 Divide the potato mixture equally into 3 medium bowls. Spoon the rutabaga into one bowl and mix thoroughly. Spoon the carrot into the second bowl and mix thoroughly. Spoon the spinach into the third bowl and mix thoroughly.

5 Add the cinnamon to the rutabaga and potato mixture and season to taste. Stir the orange juice into the carrot and potato mixture. Stir the nutmeg into the spinach and potato mixture.

6 Spoon a layer of the rutabaga and potato mixture into each of the ramekins and smooth over the top. Cover each with a layer of spinach and potato mixture, then top with the carrot and potato mixture. Cover the ramekins with foil and place in a roasting pan. Half-fill the pan with boiling water and cook in a preheated oven, 350°F/180°C, for 40 minutes, or until set.

7 Turn out onto serving plates. Garnish with the carrot batons and serve immediately.

4

6

6

caramelized new potatoes

serves four

1lb 8 oz/675 g new
  potatoes, scrubbed

4 tbsp dark brown sugar

4 tbsp butter

1 tbsp orange juice

1 tbsp chopped fresh parsley or
  cilantro

salt and pepper

orange rind curls, to garnish

VARIATION

Lemon or lime juices may be
used instead of the orange juice,
if you like. In addition, garnish
the finished dish with pared
lemon or lime rind, if you like.

1 Cook the new potatoes in a large
pan of boiling water for about
10 minutes, or until almost tender.
Drain thoroughly.

2 Melt the brown sugar in a large,
heavy skillet over low heat,
stirring constantly.

3 Add the butter and orange juice
to the skillet, stirring the mixture
constantly as the butter melts.

4 Add the potatoes to the orange
and butter mixture and continue
to cook, turning the potatoes
frequently until they are completely
coated in the caramel.

5 Sprinkle the chopped fresh parsley
or cilantro over the potatoes and
season according to taste with salt
and pepper.

6 Transfer the caramelized new
potatoes to a serving dish and
garnish with the orange rind curls.
Serve immediately.

spicy potatoes & onions

serves four

6 tbsp vegetable oil

2 medium-sized onions,
    chopped finely

1 tsp finely chopped fresh gingerroot

1 tsp crushed garlic

1 tsp chili powder

1½ tsp ground cumin

1½ tsp ground coriander

1 tsp salt

400 g/14 oz canned new potatoes

1 tbsp lemon juice

BAGHAAR

3 tbsp oil

3 dried red chiles

½ tsp onion seeds

½ tsp mustard seeds

½ tsp fenugreek seeds

TO GARNISH

fresh cilantro leaves

1 fresh green chile, seeded and
    chopped finely

1 Heat the oil in a large pan. Cook the onions, stirring, until golden brown. Reduce the heat, add the ginger, garlic, chili powder, cumin, coriander, salt, and potatoes and stir-fry for about 1 minute. Remove the pan from the heat and set aside until required.

2 Drain the water from the potatoes. Add the potatoes to the onion and spice mixture and heat through. Sprinkle in the lemon juice and mix well.

3 To make the baghaar, heat the oil in a separate pan. Add the red chiles, onion seeds, mustard seeds, and fenugreek seeds and cook until the seeds turn a shade darker. Remove the pan from the heat and pour the baghaar over the potatoes.

4 Garnish with cilantro leaves and chopped chile, then serve.

121

spicy indian potatoes

serves four

½ tsp coriander seeds

1 tsp cumin seeds

4 tbsp vegetable oil

2 cardamom pods

1 tsp grated fresh gingerroot

1 fresh red chile, seeded
    and chopped

1 onion, chopped

2 garlic cloves, crushed

1 lb/450 g new potatoes, quartered

⅔ cup vegetable bouillon

1lb 8 oz/675 g fresh spinach,
    chopped

4 tbsp plain yogurt

salt

VARIATION

Use frozen spinach instead
of fresh spinach, if you prefer.
Defrost the frozen spinach and
drain it thoroughly before adding
it to the dish, otherwise it
will turn soggy.

---

1 Grind the coriander and cumin seeds using a pestle and mortar.

2 Heat the oil in a skillet. Add the ground coriander and cumin seeds to the pan together with the cardamom pods and ginger and cook for about 2 minutes.

3 Add the chopped chile, onion, and garlic to the pan. Cook for 2 minutes more, stirring frequently.

4 Add the potatoes to the skillet together with the vegetable bouillon. Cook gently for 30 minutes, or until the potatoes are cooked through, stirring occasionally.

5 Add the spinach to the skillet and cook for 5 minutes more.

6 Remove the skillet from the heat and stir in the yogurt. Season with salt and pepper to taste. Transfer the potatoes and spinach to a serving dish and serve.

COOK'S TIP

An earthenware, marble, or cast
iron mortar and pestle is ideal for
grinding spices. You can also buy
spice mills from kitchen stores,
but these are not always easy to
clean and you can end up with a
mixture of flavors that you did
not anticipate or want.

potatoes in red wine

serves four

½ cup butter

1 lb/450 g new potatoes, halved

¾ cup red wine

6 tbsp beef bouillon

8 shallots, halved

4½ oz/125 g oyster mushrooms

1 tbsp chopped fresh sage
   or cilantro

salt and pepper

sage leaves or cilantro sprigs,
   to garnish

VARIATION

If oyster mushrooms are
unavailable, other mushrooms,
such as large open-cup
mushrooms, can be used instead.

3 Stir in the mushrooms and
chopped sage or cilantro and
cook for 5 minutes more.

4 Turn the potatoes and
mushrooms into a warm serving
dish. Garnish with fresh sage leaves or
cilantro sprigs and serve immediately.

1 Melt the butter in a heavy skillet
and add the halved potatoes.
Cook gently for about 5 minutes,
stirring constantly.

2 Add the red wine, beef bouillon,
and halved shallots. Season to
taste with salt and pepper and then
simmer for 30 minutes.

pommes anna

COOK'S TIP

Make sure that the potatoes are sliced very thinly so that they are almost transparent. This will ensure that they cook thoroughly.

1 Lightly grease a shallow 4-cup ovenproof dish with a little of the melted butter.

2 Slice the potatoes thinly and pat dry with paper towels.

3 Arrange a layer of potato slices in the prepared dish until the base is covered. Brush with a little butter and sprinkle with a fourth of the chopped mixed herbs. Season to taste.

4 Continue layering the potato slices, brushing each layer with melted butter and sprinkling with herbs, until they are all used up.

5 Brush the top layer of potato slices with butter. Cover the dish and cook in a preheated oven, 375°F/190°C, for 1½ hours.

6 Turn out onto a warm ovenproof platter and return to the oven for 25–30 minutes more, until golden brown. Serve, garnished with herbs.

broiled potatoes with lime

serves four

1 lb/450 g potatoes, unpeeled
   and scrubbed

3 tbsp butter, melted

2 tbsp chopped fresh thyme

paprika, for dusting

salt and pepper

LIME MAYONNAISE

⅔ cup mayonnaise

2 tsp lime juice

finely grated rind of 1 lime

1 garlic clove, crushed

pinch of paprika

salt and pepper

1 Cut the potatoes into ½-inch/1-cm thick slices.

2 Cook the potatoes in a pan of boiling water for 5–7 minutes; they should still be quite firm. Remove the potatoes with a slotted spoon and drain thoroughly.

3 Line a broiler pan with aluminum foil, then place the potato slices on top of the foil.

4 Brush the potatoes with the melted butter and sprinkle the chopped thyme on top. Season to taste with salt and pepper.

5 Cook the potatoes under a preheated medium broiler for 10 minutes, turning them over once.

6 Meanwhile, make the lime mayonnaise. Combine the mayonnaise, lime juice, lime rind, garlic, paprika, and salt and pepper to taste, in a bowl.

7 Dust the hot potato slices with a little paprika and transfer to a warm serving dish. Serve immediately with the bowl of lime mayonnaise for dipping.

COOK'S TIP

For an impressive side dish, thread the potato slices onto skewers and cook over a medium hot barbecue.

potatoes dauphinois

serves four

1 tbsp butter

1lb 8 oz/675 g waxy potatoes, sliced

2 garlic cloves, crushed

1 red onion, sliced

¾ cup grated Swiss cheese

1¼ cups heavy cream

salt and pepper

COOK'S TIP

There are many versions of this classic potato dish, but the different recipes always contain heavy cream, making it a rich and very filling side dish or accompaniment.

1 Lightly grease the base and sides of a 4-cup shallow ovenproof dish with the butter.

2 Arrange a single layer of potato slices in the base of the prepared dish to cover.

3 Top the potato slices with half the garlic, half the sliced red onion, and one-third of the grated Swiss cheese. Season to taste with a little salt and pepper.

4 Repeat the layers in exactly the same order, finishing with a layer of potatoes topped with grated cheese.

5 Pour the cream over the top of the potatoes and cook in a preheated oven, 350°F/180°C, for 1½ hours, or until the potatoes are cooked through and the top is browned and crisp. Serve immediately, straight from the dish.

spicy potato fries

serves four

4 large waxy potatoes

2 sweet potatoes

4 tbsp butter, melted

½ tsp chili powder

1 tsp garam masala

salt

COOK'S TIP

Rinsing the potatoes in cold water before cooking removes the starch, thus preventing them from sticking together. Soaking them in a bowl of cold salted water makes the fries crisper.

1 Cut the potatoes and sweet potatoes into slices about ½-inch/1-cm thick, then cut them into finger-shaped fries.

2 Place the potatoes in a large bowl of cold salted water. Let soak for 20 minutes.

3 Remove the potato slices with a slotted spoon and drain thoroughly. Pat with paper towels until completely dry.

4 Pour the melted butter onto a cookie sheet. Transfer the potato slices to the cookie sheet.

5 Sprinkle with the chili powder and garam masala, turning the potato slices to coat them with the mixture all over.

6 Cook the fries in a preheated oven, 400°F/200°C, turning frequently, for 40 minutes, until they are browned and cooked through.

7 Drain the fries on paper towels to remove the excess oil and then serve immediately.

lemony & herbed potatoes

LEMONY NEW POTATOES

2 lb 4 oz/1 kg new potatoes

1 oz/25 g butter

1 tbsp finely grated lemon rind

2 tbsp lemon juice

1 tbsp chopped fresh dill or chives

salt and pepper

extra chopped fresh dill or chives,
    to garnish

HERBED NEW POTATOES

2 lb 4 oz/1 kg new potatoes

3 tbsp light olive oil

1 tbsp white wine vinegar

pinch of dry mustard

pinch of superfine sugar

2 tbsp chopped mixed fresh herbs,
    such as parsley, chives,
    marjoram, basil, and rosemary

salt and pepper

extra chopped fresh mixed herbs,
    to garnish

1 For the lemony potatoes, either scrub the potatoes well or remove the skins by scraping them off with the blade of a sharp knife. Cook the potatoes in plenty of lightly salted, boiling water for about 15 minutes, until just tender.

2 While the potatoes are cooking, melt the butter over low heat. Add the lemon rind, juice, and herbs. Season with salt and pepper.

3 Drain the cooked potatoes and transfer to a serving bowl.

4 Pour over the lemony butter mixture and stir gently to mix. Garnish with extra herbs and serve hot or warm.

5 For the herbed potatoes, prepare and cook the potatoes as described in step 1. Whisk the olive oil, vinegar, mustard, sugar, and seasoning together in a small bowl. Add the chopped herbs and mix well.

6 Drain the potatoes and pour over the oil and vinegar mixture, stirring to coat evenly. Garnish with extra fresh herbs and serve warm or cold.

potatoes lyonnaise

serves six

2 lb 12 oz/1.25 kg potatoes

4 tbsp olive oil

2 tbsp butter

2 onions, sliced

2–3 garlic cloves, crushed (optional)

salt and pepper

chopped fresh parsley, to garnish

COOK'S TIP

If the potatoes blacken slightly
as they are boiling, add a
spoonful of lemon juice
to the cooking water.

1 Slice the potatoes into ¼-inch/ 5-mm slices. Put in a large pan of lightly salted water and bring to a boil. Cover and simmer gently for about 10–12 minutes, until just tender. Avoid boiling too rapidly or the potatoes will break up and lose their shape. When cooked, drain well.

2 While the potatoes are cooking, heat the oil and butter in a very large skillet. Add the onions and garlic, if using, and fry over a medium heat, stirring frequently, until the onions are softened.

3 Add the cooked potato slices to the skillet and cook with the onions and garlic, carefully stirring occasionally, for about 5–8 minutes, until the potatoes are well browned all over.

4 Season to taste with salt and pepper. Sprinkle over the chopped parsley to serve. If you like, transfer the potatoes and onions to a large ovenproof dish and keep warm in a low oven until ready to serve.

potatoes in coconut cream

serves four

1 lb 5 oz/600 g potatoes

1 onion, sliced thinly

2 fresh red bird-eye chiles, seeded
and chopped finely

½ tsp salt

½ tsp ground black pepper

½ cup coconut cream

1½ cups vegetable or chicken
bouillon

chopped fresh cilantro or basil,
to garnish

COOK'S TIP

If the potatoes are thin-skinned,
or a new variety, simply wash or
scrub to remove any dirt and
cook with the skins on. This adds
extra dietary fiber and nutrients
to the finished dish, and cuts
down on the preparation time.
Baby new potatoes can be
cooked whole.

1 Peel the potatoes thinly. Use a
sharp knife to cut into ¾-inch/
2-cm chunks.

2 Place the potatoes in a pan with
the onion, chiles, salt, pepper,
and coconut cream. Stir in the
vegetable or chicken bouillon.

3 Bring to a boil, stirring, then
lower the heat, and cover. Simmer
gently, stirring occasionally, until the
potatoes are tender.

4 Adjust the seasoning to taste,
then sprinkle with chopped
cilantro or basil. Serve immediately
while hot.

potatoes in green sauce

serves five

2 lb 4 oz/1 kg small waxy
potatoes, peeled

1 onion, halved and unpeeled

8 garlic cloves, unpeeled

1 fresh green chile

8 tomatillos, outer husks removed,
or small tart tomatoes

scant 1 cup chicken, meat, or
vegetable bouillon

½ tsp ground cumin

1 fresh thyme sprig or generous
pinch dried thyme

1 fresh oregano sprig or generous
pinch dried oregano

2 tbsp vegetable or extra virgin olive
oil

1 zucchini, chopped coarsely

1 bunch of fresh cilantro, chopped

salt

1 Put the potatoes in a pan of salted water. Bring to a boil and cook for about 15 minutes, or until almost tender. Do not overcook them. Drain and set aside.

2 Meanwhile, lightly char the onion, garlic, chile, and tomatillos or tomatoes in a heavy, ungreased skillet. Set aside, and when cool enough to handle, peel and chop the onion, garlic, and chile; chop the tomatillos or tomatoes. Put in a blender or food processor with half the bouillon and process to form a purée. Add the cumin, thyme, and oregano.

3 Heat the oil in the heavy skillet. Add the purée and cook for 5 minutes, stirring, to reduce slightly and concentrate the flavors.

4 Add the potatoes and zucchini to the spicy purée and pour in the remainder of the bouillon. Add about half the chopped cilantro and cook for 5 minutes more, or until the chopped zucchini is tender.

5 Transfer to a serving bowl and serve sprinkled with the remaining chopped cilantro to garnish.

potatoes with almonds

serves four

1lb 5oz/600 g potatoes, unpeeled
   and sliced

1 tbsp vegetable oil

1 red onion, halved and sliced

1 garlic clove, crushed

½ cup almond slivers

½ tsp ground turmeric

4½ oz/125 g arugula leaves

1¼ cups heavy cream

salt and pepper

1 Cook the sliced potatoes in a pan of boiling water for 10 minutes. Drain them thoroughly.

2 Heat the vegetable oil in a heavy skillet. Add the onion and garlic and cook over medium heat, stirring frequently, for 3–4 minutes.

3 Add the almonds, turmeric, and potato slices to the skillet and cook, stirring constantly, for about 2–3 minutes. Stir in the arugula leaves.

4 Transfer the potato and almond mixture to a shallow ovenproof dish. Pour the heavy cream evenly over the top and season to taste with salt and pepper.

5 Cook in a preheated oven, 375°F/ 190°C, for 20 minutes, or until the potatoes are cooked through. Transfer to a warmed serving dish and serve them immediately.

baked potatoes & mushrooms

serves four

2 tbsp butter

1 lb 2 oz/500 g waxy potatoes,
 sliced thinly

2 cups sliced mixed mushrooms

1 tbsp chopped fresh rosemary

4 tbsp chopped fresh chives

2 garlic cloves, crushed

⅔ cup heavy cream

salt and pepper

chopped fresh chives, to garnish

1 Grease a shallow, round, ovenproof dish with butter.

2 Parboil the sliced potatoes in a pan of boiling water for 10 minutes. Drain well. Layer a quarter of the potatoes in the base of the dish.

3 Arrange a fourth of the mushrooms on top of the potatoes and sprinkle with a fourth of the rosemary, chives, and garlic. Continue making layers in the same order, finishing with a layer of potatoes on top.

4 Pour the cream over the top of the potatoes. Season to taste with salt and pepper.

5 Cook in a preheated oven, 375°F/190°C, for about 45 minutes, or until the topping is golden brown and piping hot.

6 Garnish with chopped fresh chives and serve immediately straight from the dish.

cheese & potato slices

serves four

2 lb/900 g large waxy potatoes,
   unpeeled and sliced thickly
1 cup fresh white bread crumbs
½ cup grated Parmesan cheese
1½ tsp chili powder
2 eggs, beaten
vegetable oil, for deep frying
chili powder, for dusting (optional)

COOK'S TIP
The cheese and potato slices may
be coated in the bread crumb
mixture in advance and then
stored in the refrigerator until
ready to use.

1 Cook the sliced potatoes in a pan
of boiling water for about 10–15
minutes, or until the potatoes are just
tender. Drain thoroughly.

2 Combine the bread crumbs,
cheese, and chili powder in a
bowl, then transfer to a shallow dish.
Pour the beaten eggs into a separate
shallow dish.

3 Dip the potato slices first in egg
and then roll them in the bread
crumbs to coat completely.

4 Heat the oil in a large, heavy pan
to 350–375°F/180–190°C or until
a cube of bread browns in 30 seconds.
Add the cheese and potato slices, in
several batches, and cook for about
4–5 minutes, or until a golden brown
color all over.

5 Remove the cheese and potato
slices from the oil with a slotted
spoon and drain thoroughly on paper
towels. Keep the cheese and potato
slices warm while you cook the
remaining batches.

6 Transfer the cheese and potato
slices to warm individual serving
plates. Dust lightly with chili powder, if
using, and serve immediately.

fried potatoes with onions

serves four

2 lb/900 g waxy potatoes, diced

½ cup butter

1 red onion, cut into 8 wedges

2 garlic cloves, crushed

1 tsp lemon juice

2 tbsp chopped fresh thyme

salt and pepper

1 Cook the diced potatoes in a pan of boiling water for 10 minutes. Drain them thoroughly.

2 Melt the butter in a large, heavy skillet and add the red onion wedges, garlic, and lemon juice. Cook for 2–3 minutes, stirring.

3 Add the potatoes to the skillet and mix well to coat all over in the butter mixture.

4 Reduce the heat to low, then cover the skillet, and cook for 25–30 minutes, or until the potatoes are golden and tender.

5 Sprinkle the chopped thyme over the top of the potatoes and season with salt and pepper to taste.

6 Serve immediately as a side dish to accompany broiled meats or fish.

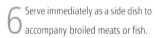

spiced potatoes & spinach

serves four

3 tbsp vegetable oil

1 red onion, sliced

2 garlic cloves, crushed

½ tsp chili powder

2 tsp ground coriander

1 tsp ground cumin

⅔ cup vegetable bouillon

1¾ cups potatoes, diced

1 lb 2 oz/500 g baby spinach

1 fresh red chile, seeded
    and sliced

salt and pepper

1 Heat the oil in a heavy skillet. Add the onion and garlic and sauté over medium heat, stirring occasionally, for 2–3 minutes.

2 Stir in the chili powder, ground coriander, and ground cumin, and cook, stirring constantly, for about 30 seconds.

COOK'S TIP
Besides adding extra color to a dish, red onions have a sweeter, less pungent flavor than other varieties.

3 Add the vegetable bouillon, diced potatoes, and spinach, and bring to a boil. Reduce the heat, cover the skillet, and simmer gently for about 10 minutes, or until the potatoes are cooked right through and tender.

4 Uncover and season to taste with salt and pepper, then add the red chile and cook for 2–3 minutes. Transfer the spiced potatoes and spinach to a warmed serving dish and serve immediately.

potatoes, olives & anchovies

serves four

1 lb/450 g baby new
    potatoes, scrubbed

¾ cup mixed olives

8 canned anchovy fillets, drained

2 tbsp olive oil

2 fennel bulbs, trimmed
    and sliced

2 fresh rosemary sprigs,
    stalks removed

salt

COOK'S TIP

Fresh rosemary is particularly
popular with Italians, but you
can experiment with your
favorite herbs in this recipe,
if you like.

1 Bring a large pan of lightly salted water to a boil. Add the potatoes, bring back to a boil, and simmer over medium heat for 8–10 minutes, or until tender. Remove the potatoes from the pan using a slotted spoon and set aside to cool slightly.

2 Once the potatoes are cool enough to handle, cut them into wedges, using a sharp knife.

3 Pit the mixed olives with a cherry pitter or small, sharp knife and cut them in half.

4 Using a sharp knife, chop the anchovy fillets into thinner strips or chop.

5 Heat the olive oil in a large, heavy skillet. Add the potato wedges, sliced fennel, and rosemary. Cook over medium heat, stirring occasionally, for 7–8 minutes, or until the potatoes are golden.

6 Stir in the mixed olives and the anchovies and cook, stirring occasionally, for 1 minute, or until completely warmed through.

7 Transfer the potato mixture to warmed serving plates and serve.

italian potato wedges

serves four

2 large waxy potatoes, unpeeled

4 large ripe tomatoes, skinned
    and seeded

²⁄₃ cup vegetable bouillon

2 tbsp tomato paste

1 small yellow bell pepper, seeded
    and cut into strips

4½ oz/125 g white mushrooms, cut
    into quarters

1 tbsp chopped fresh basil

½ cup grated cheese

salt and pepper

1 Cut each of the potatoes into 8 equal wedges. Parboil the potatoes in a pan of boiling water for 15 minutes. Drain well and place in a shallow ovenproof dish.

2 Coarsely chop the tomatoes and add to the dish. Combine the vegetable bouillon and tomato paste in a bowl or pitcher, stirring well to mix, then pour the mixture over the potatoes and tomatoes.

3 Add the yellow bell pepper strips, mushroom quarters, and chopped basil, then season to taste with salt and pepper.

4 Sprinkle the grated cheese evenly over the top and cook in a preheated oven, 375°F/190°C, for 15–20 minutes until the topping is golden brown and bubbling. Serve immediately, straight from the dish.

potatoes with goat cheese

serves four

2 lb 12 oz/1.25 kg baking potatoes,
   peeled and cut into chunks

pinch of salt

pinch of sugar

¾ cup sour cream

1 cup vegetable or chicken bouillon

3 garlic cloves, chopped finely

a few shakes of bottled chipotle
   salsa, or 1 dried chipotle,
   rehydrated, seeded, and
   sliced thinly

8 oz/225 g goat cheese, sliced

1½ cups mozzarella or Cheddar
   cheese, grated

scant ⅔ cup grated Parmesan or
   romano cheese

salt

1 Put the potatoes in a large pan of water with the salt and sugar. Bring to a boil, lower the heat and cook for about 10 minutes, until they are half cooked.

2 Combine the crème fraîche with the vegetable or chicken bouillon, garlic, and chipotle salsa or rehydrated dried chile in a bowl.

3 Arrange half the potatoes in a casserole. Pour half the crème fraîche sauce over the potatoes and cover with the goat cheese. Top with the remaining potatoes and the sauce.

4 Sprinkle with the grated mozzarella or Cheddar cheese, then with either the grated Parmesan or romano.

5 Bake in a preheated oven, 350°F/ 180°C for about 25 minutes, or until the potatoes are tender and the cheese topping is lightly golden and crisped in places. Serve immediately, straight from the casserole.

145

souffléed cheesy potato fries

serves four

2 lb/900 g potatoes, cut into chunks

²/₃ cup heavy cream

¾ cup grated Swiss cheese

pinch of cayenne pepper

2 egg whites

vegetable oil, for deep-frying

salt and pepper

chopped fresh flatleaf parsley and
    grated cheese, to garnish

VARIATION

Add other flavorings, such as
grated nutmeg or curry powder,
to the cream and cheese.

COOK'S TIP

Swiss cheese has a sweet,
nutty flavor and melts well.
Look for the genuine product,
which will have "Switzerland"
stamped all over the rind. It
should have only a sprinkling of
small holes.

---

1 Cook the potatoes in a pan of lightly salted, boiling water for about 10 minutes. Drain thoroughly and pat dry with absorbent paper towels. Set aside until required.

2 Mix the heavy cream and Swiss cheese in a large bowl. Stir in the cayenne pepper and season with salt and pepper to taste.

3 Whisk the egg whites until stiff peaks form. Gently fold into the cheese mixture until fully incorporated.

4 Add the cooked potatoes, turning to coat thoroughly in the mixture.

5 In a deep pan, heat the oil to 350–375°F/180–190°C or until a cube of bread browns in 30 seconds. Remove the potatoes from the cheese mixture with a slotted spoon and cook in the oil, in batches if necessary, for 3–4 minutes, or until golden.

6 Transfer the potatoes to a warmed serving dish and garnish with flatleaf parsley and grated cheese. Serve immediately.

chili roast potatoes

serves four

500 g/1 lb 2 oz small new
   potatoes, scrubbed
⅔ cup vegetable oil
1 tsp chili powder
½ tsp caraway seeds
1 tsp salt
1 tbsp chopped fresh basil

VARIATION

Use any other spice of your
choice, such as curry powder or
paprika, for a variation in flavor.

1 Cook the potatoes in a pan of boiling water for 10 minutes, then drain them thoroughly.

2 Pour a little of the oil into a shallow roasting pan to coat the base. Heat the oil in a preheated oven, 400°F/200°C, for 10 minutes. Add the potatoes to the pan and brush them with the hot oil.

3 In a small bowl, combine the chili powder, caraway seeds, and salt. Sprinkle the mixture over the potatoes, turning to coat them all over.

4 Add the remaining oil to the pan and roast in the oven for about 15 minutes, or until the potatoes are cooked through.

5 Using a slotted spoon, remove the potatoes from the the oil, draining them thoroughly, and transfer them to a warmed serving dish. Sprinkle the chopped basil over the top and serve immediately.

parmesan potatoes

serves four

3 lb/1.3 kg potatoes

scant ⅔ cup grated Parmesan
cheese

pinch of freshly grated nutmeg

1 tbsp chopped fresh parsley

vegetable oil, for roasting

4 smoked bacon strips, cut into
thin strips

salt

1 Cut the potatoes in half lengthwise and cook them in a pan of lightly salted, boiling water for 10 minutes. Drain them thoroughly.

2 Combine the grated Parmesan cheese, nutmeg, and parsley in a shallow bowl.

3 Roll the potato pieces in the cheese mixture to coat them completely. Shake off any excess.

4 Pour a little oil into a roasting pan and heat it in a preheated oven, 400°F/200°C, for 10 minutes. Remove from the oven and place the potatoes into the pan. Return to the oven and cook for 30 minutes, turning once.

5 Remove from the oven and sprinkle the bacon on top of the potatoes. Return to the oven for 15 minutes, or until the potatoes and bacon are cooked. Drain off any excess fat and serve.

VARIATION

If you like, use slices of salami or prosciutto instead of the bacon, adding it to the dish 5 minutes before the end of the cooking time.

mini vegetable puff pastries

serves four

PASTRY

1 lb/450 g puff pastry, thawed
if frozen

all-purpose flour, for dusting

1 egg, beaten

FILLING

8 oz/225 g sweet potatoes, diced

3½ oz/100 g baby asparagus spears

2 tbsp butter or margarine

1 leek, sliced

2 open-cup mushrooms, sliced

1 tsp lime juice

1 tsp chopped fresh thyme

pinch of mustard powder

salt and pepper

COOK'S TIP

Making puff pastry yourself is not difficult, but is immensely time-consuming because it involves a process of rolling, folding, and chilling that is repeated several times. Ready-made puff pastry, either frozen or chilled, is usually of good quality and is certainly more convenient for the busy cook.

1 Cut the pastry into 4 equal pieces. Roll each piece out on a lightly floured surface to form a 5-inch/13-cm square. Place the pieces on a dampened cookie sheet and score a smaller 2.5-inch/6-cm square inside.

2 Brush with beaten egg and cook in a preheated oven, 400°F/200°C, for 20 minutes, or until risen and golden brown.

VARIATION

Use a colorful selection of any vegetables you have at hand for this recipe.

3 While the pastry is cooking, start the filling. Cook the sweet potato in a pan of boiling water for 15 minutes, then drain well. Blanch the asparagus in a pan of boiling water for 10 minutes, or until tender. Drain well and reserve.

4 Remove the pastry squares from the oven. Cut out the central square of pastry and lift out. Reserve.

5 Melt the butter or margarine in a pan and sauté the leek and mushrooms for 2–3 minutes. Add the lime juice, thyme, and mustard and season well. Stir in the sweet potatoes and asparagus. Spoon into the pastry cases. Top with the reserved pastry squares and serve immediately.

pesto potatoes

serves four

2 lb/900 g small new potatoes

2¾ oz/75 g fresh basil

2 tbsp pine nuts

3 garlic cloves, crushed

½ cup olive oil

¾ cup freshly grated Parmesan cheese
    and romano cheese, mixed

salt and pepper

fresh basil sprigs, to garnish

1 Cook the potatoes in a pan of salted boiling water for 15 minutes, or until tender. Drain well, transfer to a warm serving dish, and keep warm until required.

2 Meanwhile, put the basil, pine nuts, garlic, and a little salt and pepper to taste in a food processor. Blend for 30 seconds, then add the oil gradually, processing until the mixture is smooth.

3 Remove the mixture from the food processor and place in a mixing bowl. Stir in the grated Parmesan and romano cheeses and mix together.

4 Spoon the pesto sauce over the potatoes and toss lightly and carefully so that the potatoes are thoroughly coated. Garnish with fresh basil sprigs and serve the pesto potatoes immediately.

bombay potatoes

serves four

2 lb 4 oz/1 kg waxy potatoes

2 tbsp vegetable ghee

1 tsp panch poran spice mix

3 tsp ground turmeric

2 tbsp tomato paste

1¼ cups plain yogurt

salt

chopped fresh cilantro, to garnish

COOK'S TIP

Panch poran spice mix is made from equal quantities of cumin , fennel, mustard, nigella, and fenugreek seeds.

---

1 Put the whole potatoes into a large pan of salted cold water. Bring to a boil, then simmer until the potatoes are just cooked, but not tender; the time depends on the size of the potato, but an average-size one should take about 15 minutes.

2 Heat the ghee in a separate pan over a medium heat and add the panch poran, turmeric, tomato paste, yogurt, and salt. Bring to a boil and simmer, uncovered, for 5 minutes.

3 Drain the potatoes and cut each one into 4 pieces. Add the potatoes to the pan, then cover, and cook briefly. Transfer to an ovenproof casserole. Cook in a preheated oven, 350°F/180°C, for about 40 minutes, or until the potatoes are tender and the sauce has thickened a little.

4 Sprinkle with chopped cilantro to garnish and serve the Bombay potatoes immediately.

crispy potato skins

serves four

8 small baking potatoes, scrubbed

4 tbsp butter, melted

salt and pepper

OPTIONAL TOPPING

6 scallions, sliced

½ cup grated Swiss cheese

1¾ oz/50 g salami, cut into
thin strips

COOK'S TIP

Potato skins can be served on their own, but they are delicious served with a dip. Try a spicy tomato or hummus dip.

1 Prick the potatoes with a fork and bake in a preheated oven, 400°F/200°C, for 1 hour or until tender.

2 Cut the potatoes in half and carefully scoop out the flesh with a teaspoon, leaving about ¼-inch/5-mm potato flesh lining the skin.

3 Generously brush the melted butter all over the insides of the potato skins.

4 Place the skins, cut side down, over medium hot coals on a barbecue for 10–15 minutes. Alternatively, cook under a preheated broiler for 10–15 minutes.

5 Turn the potato skins over and cook on the barbecue or under the broiler for 5 minutes more, or until they are crisp. Take care that they do not burn.

6 Season the potato skins with salt and pepper to taste and serve while they are still warm.

7 If you like, the skins can be filled with a variety of toppings. Cook the potato skins as above for about 10 minutes, then turn cut side up and sprinkle with slices of scallion, grated cheese, and salami strips. Cook for 5 minutes more, until the cheese begins to melt. Serve hot.

paprika crisps

serves four

2 large potatoes

3 tbsp olive oil

½ tsp paprika

salt

1 Using a sharp knife, slice the potatoes very thinly so that they are almost transparent. Place in a bowl of cold water. Drain the potato slices and pat dry with paper towels.

2 Heat the oil in a large, heavy skillet and add the paprika. Cook over low heat, stirring constantly to make sure that the paprika doesn't catch light and burn onto the base of the skillet.

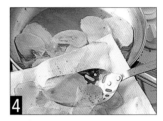

3 Add the potato slices to the skillet and cook them in a single layer for about 5 minutes, or until the potato slices are just beginning to curl slightly at the edges.

4 Remove the potato slices from the skillet using a slotted spoon and transfer them to paper towels to drain thoroughly.

5 Thread the potato slices onto several wooden kabob skewers.

6 Sprinkle the potato slices with a salt and cook over a medium hot barbecue grill or under medium broiler, turning frequently, for 10 minutes, until they begin to crisp. Sprinkle with a little more salt and serve immediately.

chinese potato sticks

serves four

1 lb 7 oz/650 g medium potatoes

8 tbsp vegetable oil

1 fresh red chile, seeded
    and halved

1 small onion, quartered

2 garlic cloves, halved

2 tbsp light soy sauce

pinch of salt

1 tsp wine vinegar

1 tbsp coarse sea salt

pinch of chili powder

1 Peel the potatoes and cut into thin slices along their length. Cut the slices into very thin sticks.

2 Bring a pan of water to a boil and blanch the potato sticks for 2 minutes. Drain and rinse under cold water, then drain well again. Pat the potato sticks thoroughly dry with paper towels.

3 Heat the oil in a preheated wok until it is almost smoking. Add the chile, onion, and garlic and stir-fry for 30 seconds. Remove and discard the chile, onion, and garlic.

4 Add the potato sticks to the oil and fry for 3–4 minutes, or until golden brown.

5 Add the soy sauce, salt, and vinegar to the wok. Reduce the heat and cook for 1 minute, or until the potatoes are crisp.

6 Remove the potatoes with a slotted spoon and drain well on paper towels.

7 Transfer the potato sticks to a serving dish. Sprinkle with the sea salt and chili powder and serve.

garlic potato wedges

serves four

3 large baking potatoes, scrubbed

4 tbsp olive oil

2 tbsp butter

2 garlic cloves, chopped

1 tbsp chopped fresh rosemary

1 tbsp chopped fresh parsley

1 tbsp chopped fresh thyme

salt and pepper

COOK'S TIP
You may find it easier to grill these potatoes in a hinged rack

1 Bring a large pan of water to a boil. Add the potatoes and parboil them for 10 minutes. Drain the potatoes and refresh under cold water, then drain them again thoroughly.

2 Transfer the potatoes to a cutting board. When the potatoes are cold enough to handle, cut them into thick wedges, but do not peel.

3 Heat the oil and butter in a small pan together with the garlic. Cook gently over low heat until the garlic begins to brown, then remove the pan from the heat.

4 Stir the herbs into the mixture in the pan and season to taste with salt and pepper.

5 Brush the herb mixture all over the potato wedges.

6 Grill the potatoes over hot coals for 10–15 minutes, brushing liberally with any of the remaining herb and butter mixture, or until the potato wedges are just tender.

7 Transfer the garlic potato wedges to a warm serving plate and serve as an appetizer or as a side dish.

Meat & Poultry

This chapter contains a wide selection of delicious main meal dishes. The potato is the main ingredient in the majority of these recipes, but there are also ideas for adding meat, poultry, fish, and vegetables, so that there is sure to be something for everyone. The recipes come from all around the world—try Potato Ravioli or Lamb & Potato Masala. There are also hearty dishes, including creamy Chicken & Potato Casserole, and Shepherd's Pie. Whatever the occasion, you are sure to find something here to entice you.

potato ravioli

serves four

FILLING

1 tbsp vegetable oil

4½ oz/125 g ground beef

1 shallot, diced

1 garlic clove, crushed

1 tbsp all-purpose flour

1 tbsp tomato paste

⅔ cup beef bouillon

1 celery stalk, chopped

2 tomatoes, skinned and diced

2 tsp chopped fresh basil

salt and pepper

RAVIOLI

2⅔ cups diced mealy potatoes

3 medium egg yolks

3 tbsp olive oil

1½ cups all-purpose flour, plus extra
    for dusting

5 tbsp butter, for frying

salt and pepper

shredded basil leaves, to garnish

1 To make the filling, heat the oil in a pan and cook the beef for 3–4 minutes, breaking it up with a spoon. Add the shallot and garlic and cook for 2–3 minutes, until the shallot has softened.

2 Stir in the flour and tomato paste and cook for 1 minute. Stir in the beef bouillon, celery, tomatoes, and the chopped fresh basil. Season to taste with salt and pepper.

3 Cook the mixture over low heat for 20 minutes. Remove from the heat and let cool.

4 To make the ravioli, cook the potatoes in a pan of boiling water for 10 minutes, until tender.

5 Mash the potatoes in a mixing bowl. Add the egg yolks and oil. Season, then stir in the flour and mix to form a dough.

6 On a lightly floured surface, divide the dough into 24 pieces and shape into flat circles. Spoon the filling onto one half of each circle and fold the dough over to encase the filling, pressing down to seal the edges.

7 Melt the butter in a skillet and cook the ravioli, in batches, for 6–8 minutes, turning once, until golden. Serve hot, garnished with shredded basil leaves.

potato, beef & peanut pot

serves four

1 tbsp vegetable oil

5 tbsp butter

1 lb/450 g lean beef steak, cut into
thin strips

1 onion, halved and sliced

2 garlic cloves, crushed

1 lb 5 oz/600 g waxy
potatoes, diced

½ tsp paprika

4 tbsp crunchy peanut butter

2½ cups beef bouillon

¼ cup unsalted peanuts

2 tsp light soy sauce

1¾ oz/50 g snow peas

1 red bell pepper, seeded and cut
into strips

fresh parsley sprigs, to garnish

1 Heat the oil and butter in a
flameproof casserole dish.

2 Add the beef strips and cook
them gently for 3–4 minutes,
stirring and turning the meat until it is
sealed on all sides.

3 Add the onion and garlic and
cook gently for 2 minutes more,
stirring constantly.

4 Add the diced potatoes and cook
for 3–4 minutes, or until they
begin to brown slightly.

5 Stir in the paprika and peanut
butter, then gradually blend in the
beef bouillon. Bring the mixture to a
boil, stirring frequently.

6 Finally, add the peanuts, soy
sauce, snow peas, and red bell
pepper strips.

7 Cover and cook over low heat for
45 minutes, or until the beef is
cooked right through.

8 Garnish the dish with parsley
sprigs and serve immediately.

potato & meat phyllo packets

serves four

8 oz/225 g waxy potatoes,
   diced finely

1 tbsp vegetable oil

4 oz/115 g ground beef

1 leek, sliced

1 small yellow bell pepper, seeded
   and diced finely

1⅔ cups sliced white mushrooms

1 tbsp all-purpose flour

1 tbsp tomato paste

6 tbsp red wine

6 tbsp beef bouillon

1 tbsp chopped fresh rosemary

8 oz/225 g phyllo pastry, thawed
   if frozen

2 tbsp butter, melted

salt and pepper

1 Cook the diced potatoes in a pan of boiling water for 5 minutes. Drain and set aside.

2 Meanwhile, heat the oil in a pan and cook the ground beef, leek, yellow bell pepper, and mushrooms over low heat for 5 minutes.

3 Stir in the flour and tomato paste and cook for 1 minute. Gradually add the red wine and beef bouillon, stirring to thicken. Add the chopped rosemary, season to taste with salt and pepper, and set aside to cool slightly.

4 Lay 4 sheets of phyllo pastry on a counter or board. Brush each sheet with butter and lay a second layer of phyllo on top. Trim the sheets to make 4 x 8-inch/20-cm squares.

5 Brush the edges of the pastry with a little butter. Spoon a fourth of the beef mixture into the center of each square. Bring up the corners and the sides of the squares to form a packet, scrunching the edges together. Make sure that the packets are well sealed by pressing the pastry together, otherwise the filling will leak.

6 Place the packets on a cookie sheet and brush with butter. Bake in a preheated oven, 350°F/ 180°C, for 20 minutes. Serve hot.

165

potato, beef & kidney pie

serves four

8 oz/225 g waxy potatoes, diced

2 tbsp butter

1 lb/450 g lean steak, diced

5½ oz/150 g ox kidney, cored
   and chopped

12 shallots

2½ tbsp all-purpose flour, plus extra
   for dusting

⅔ cup beef bouillon

⅔ cup stout

8 oz/225 g ready-made puff pastry,
   thawed if frozen

1 egg, beaten

salt and pepper

1 Cook the diced potatoes in a pan of boiling water for 10 minutes. Drain thoroughly.

2 Meanwhile, melt the butter in a pan and add the diced steak and the kidney. Cook over medium heat for 5 minutes, stirring until the meat is sealed on all sides.

3 Add the shallots and cook for 3–4 minutes more. Stir in the flour and cook for 1 minute. Gradually stir in the beef bouillon and stout and bring to a boil, stirring constantly.

4 Stir the potatoes into the meat mixture and season to taste with salt and pepper. Reduce the heat until the mixture is just simmering gently. Cover the pan and cook for 1 hour, stirring occasionally.

5 Spoon the beef mixture into the base of a pie dish. Roll out the pastry on a lightly floured counter to an oval ½-inch /1-cm larger than the top of the dish.

6 Cut a strip of pastry long enough and wide enough to fit around the edge of the dish. Brush the edge of the dish with beaten egg and press the pastry strip around the edge. Brush with egg and place the pastry lid on top. Crimp to seal the edge and then knock up the edge with the back of a knife blade. Brush the pastry lid with beaten egg to glaze.

7 Cook the pie in a preheated oven, 450°F/230°C, for 20–25 minutes, or until the pastry has risen and is golden brown. Serve immediately, straight from the dish.

carrot-topped beef pie

serves four

1 lb/450 g lean ground beef

1 onion, chopped

1 garlic clove, crushed

1 tbsp all-purpose flour

1¼ cups beef bouillon

2 tbsp tomato paste

1 celery stalk, chopped

3 tbsp chopped fresh parsley

1 tbsp Worcestershire sauce

4 cups mealy diced potatoes

2 large carrots, diced

2 tbsp butter

3 tbsp skim milk

salt and pepper

1 Dry-fry the beef in a large pan set over high heat for 3–4 minutes, or until sealed. Add the onion and garlic and cook for 5 minutes more, stirring.

2 Add the flour and cook for 1 minute. Gradually blend in the beef bouillon and tomato paste. Stir in the celery, 1 tablespoon of the parsley, and the Worcestershire sauce. Season to taste with salt and pepper.

3 Bring the mixture to a boil, then reduce the heat, and simmer for 20–25 minutes. Spoon the beef mixture into a 5-cup pie dish.

4 Meanwhile, cook the potatoes and carrots in a pan of boiling water for 10 minutes. Drain thoroughly and mash them together.

5 Stir the butter, milk, and the remaining parsley into the potato and carrot mixture, and season with salt and pepper to taste. Spoon the potato on top of the beef mixture to cover it completely; alternatively, pipe the potato on top with a pastry bag.

6 Cook the carrot-topped beef pie in a preheated oven, 375°F/ 190°C, for 45 minutes, or until cooked through. Serve piping hot.

potato, beef & leek turnovers

serves four

8 oz/225 g diced waxy potatoes

1 small carrot, diced

8 oz/225 g beef steak, diced

1 leek, sliced

8 oz/225 g ready-made
    unsweetened shortcrust pastry,
    thawed if frozen

1 tbsp butter

1 egg, beaten

salt and pepper

crisp salad or onion gravy,
    to serve

1 Lightly grease a cookie sheet. Mix the potatoes, carrots, beef, and leek in a large bowl. Season well with salt and pepper.

2 Divide the pastry into 4 equal portions. On a lightly floured surface, roll each portion into an 8-inch/20-cm circle.

3 Spoon the potato mixture onto the center of each circle. Top the potato mixture with the butter, dividing it equally between the circles. Brush the pastry edge with a little of the beaten egg.

4 Fold the pastry over to encase the filling and crimp the edges together to seal.

5 Transfer the turnovers to the prepared cookie sheet and brush them with the beaten egg.

6 Cook in a preheated oven, 400°F/ 200°C, for 20 minutes. Reduce the oven temperature to 325°F/160°C and cook the pasties for 30 minutes more, until cooked.

7 Serve the turnovers with a crisp salad or onion gravy.

shepherd's pie

serves four–five

1 lb 9 oz/700 g lean ground lamb
  or beef

2 onions, chopped

8 oz/225 g carrots, diced

1–2 garlic cloves, crushed

1 tbsp all-purpose flour

scant 1 cup beef bouillon

7 oz/200 g canned
  chopped tomatoes

1 tsp Worcestershire sauce

1 tsp chopped fresh sage or
  oregano or ½ tsp dried sage
  or oregano

1 lb 8 oz–2 lb/675 g–1 kg potatoes

2 tbsp butter or margarine

3–4 tbsp skim milk

1¾ cups sliced white
  mushrooms, optional

salt and pepper

VARIATION

A mixture of boiled potatoes and
parsnips or rutabaga may be
used for the topping.

---

1 Place the meat in a heavy pan
with no extra fat and cook gently,
stirring frequently, until the meat
begins to brown.

2 Add the onions, carrots, and
garlic and continue to cook gently
for about 10 minutes. Stir in the flour
and cook for 1–2 minutes, then
gradually stir in the beef bouillon and
tomatoes, and bring to a boil.

3 Add the Worcestershire sauce,
herbs and seasoning, cover the
pan, and simmer gently for about
25 minutes, stirring occasionally.

4 Cook the potatoes in lightly
salted, boiling water until tender,
then drain thoroughly, and mash,
beating in the butter or margarine,
seasoning, and sufficient milk to give a
piping consistency. Place in a pastry
bag fitted with a large star tip.

5 Stir the mushrooms, if using, into
the meat, taste and adjust the
seasoning, if necessary. Turn into a
shallow ovenproof dish.

6 Pipe the potatoes evenly over the
meat. Cook in a preheated oven,
400°F/200°C for about 30 minutes,
until piping hot and the potatoes are
golden brown. Serve immediately.

lamb & potato moussaka

serves four

1 large eggplant, sliced

1 tbsp olive or vegetable oil

1 onion, chopped finely

1 garlic clove, crushed

12 oz/350 g lean ground lamb

3⅔ cups sliced mushrooms

15 oz/425 g canned chopped
  tomatoes with herbs

⅔ cup lamb or
  vegetable bouillon

2 tbsp cornstarch

2 tbsp water

1 lb 2 oz/500 g potatoes,
  parboiled for 10 minutes
  and sliced

2 eggs

½ cup soft cheese

⅔ cup plain yogurt

½ cup grated sharp
  Cheddar cheese

salt and pepper

fresh flatleaf parsley,
  to garnish

salad greens,
  to serve

1 Lay the eggplant slices on a clean surface and sprinkle liberally with salt, to extract the bitter juices. Leave for 10 minutes, then turn the slices over, and repeat. Put in a colander, rinse thoroughly, and drain well.

2 Meanwhile, heat the oil in a pan and cook the onion and garlic for 3–4 minutes. Add the lamb and mushrooms and cook for 5 minutes, until browned. Stir in the tomatoes and bouillon, bring to a boil, and simmer for 10 minutes. Mix the cornstarch with the water to a smooth paste and stir into the pan. Cook, stirring constantly, until thickened.

3 Spoon half the mixture into an ovenproof dish. Cover with the eggplant slices, then the remaining lamb mixture. Arrange the sliced potatoes on top.

4 Beat together the eggs, soft cheese and yogurt and season to taste with salt and pepper. Pour over the potatoes to cover them completely. Sprinkle with the grated cheese.

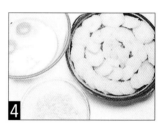

5 Bake in a preheated oven, 375°F/ 190°C for 45 minutes, until the topping is set and golden brown. Garnish with flatleaf parsley and serve with salad greens.

curried stir-fried lamb

serves four

2⅔ cups diced potatoes

1 lb/450 g lean lamb, diced

2 tbsp medium-hot curry paste

3 tbsp sunflower oil

1 onion, sliced

1 eggplant, diced

2 garlic cloves, crushed

1 tbsp grated fresh gingerroot

⅔ cup lamb or beef bouillon

salt

2 tbsp chopped fresh cilantro,
    to garnish

COOK'S TIP

The wok is an ancient Chinese
invention, the name coming from
the Cantonese word for a
cooking vessel.

VARIATION

Substitute diced skinless,
boneless chicken breast portions
for the lamb and use chicken
bouillon instead of lamb or beef.

1 Bring a large pan of lightly salted water to a boil. Add the potatoes and simmer gently for 10 minutes, until tender. Remove the potatoes from the pan with a slotted spoon and drain thoroughly.

2 Meanwhile, place the lamb in a large mixing bowl. Add the curry paste and mix well until the lamb is evenly coated in the paste.

3 Heat the sunflower oil in a large preheated wok.

4 Add the onion, eggplant, garlic, and ginger to the wok and stir-fry for about 5 minutes.

5 Add the lamb to the wok and stir-fry for 5 minutes more.

6 Add the bouillon and cooked potatoes to the wok. Bring to a boil, lower the heat, and simmer gently for 30 minutes, or until the lamb is tender and cooked through.

7 Transfer the mixture to warm serving dishes and sprinkle with chopped cilantro. Serve immediately.

lamb & potato masala

serves four

1 lb 10 oz/750 g lean lamb (from
the leg)

3 tbsp ghee or vegetable oil

1 lb 2 oz/500 g potatoes,
peeled and cut in 1-inch/
2.5-cm pieces

1 large onion, peeled, cut into
quarters, and sliced

2 garlic cloves, crushed

2½ cups thickly sliced mushrooms

10 oz/280 g ready-made Tikka
Masala Curry Sauce

1¼ cups water

3 tomatoes, halved and
sliced thinly

4½ oz/125 g spinach, washed and
stalks trimmed

salt

fresh mint sprigs,
to garnish

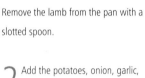

1 Cut the lamb into 1-inch/2.5-cm cubes. Heat the ghee or oil in a large pan, add the lamb and cook over moderate heat, stirring frequently for 3 minutes, or until sealed all over. Remove the lamb from the pan with a slotted spoon.

2 Add the potatoes, onion, garlic, and mushrooms and cook for 3–4 minutes, stirring frequently.

3 Stir the curry sauce and water into the pan, add the lamb, mix well, and season with salt to taste. Cover and cook very gently for 1 hour, or until the lamb is tender and cooked through, stirring occasionally.

4 Add the sliced tomatoes and the spinach to the pan, pushing the spinach leaves well down into the mixture, then cover and cook for 10 minutes more, until the spinach is cooked and tender.

5 Garnish with mint sprigs and serve hot.

meatballs in spicy sauce

serves four

8 oz/225 g mealy potatoes, diced

8 oz/225 g ground beef or lamb

1 onion, chopped finely

1 tbsp chopped fresh cilantro

1 celery stalk, chopped finely

2 garlic cloves, crushed

2 tbsp butter

1 tbsp vegetable oil

salt and pepper

chopped fresh cilantro, to garnish

SAUCE

1 tbsp vegetable oil

1 onion, chopped finely

2 tsp brown sugar

14 oz/400 g canned
    chopped tomatoes

1 fresh green chile, seeded
    and chopped

1 tsp paprika

⅔ cup vegetable bouillon

2 tsp cornstarch

1 Cook the diced potatoes in a pan of boiling water for 25 minutes, until cooked through. Drain well and transfer to a large mixing bowl. Mash until smooth.

2 Add the ground beef or lamb, onion, cilantro, celery, garlic, and seasoning and mix together well.

3 Bring the mixture together with your hands and roll it into 20 small balls.

4 To make the sauce, heat the vegetable oil in a pan and sauté the onion for 5 minutes. Add the remaining sauce ingredients and bring to a boil, stirring constantly. Lower the heat and simmer for 20 minutes.

5 Meanwhile, heat the butter and oil for the meatballs in a heavy skillet. Add the meatballs, in batches, and cook, turning frequently, for

10–15 minutes, until browned all over. Keep warm while cooking the remainder. Serve the meatballs in a warm, shallow dish with the sauce poured around them and garnished with the fresh cilantro.

spanish potatoes

serves four

4 cups diced waxy potatoes

3 tbsp olive oil

1 onion, halved and sliced

2 garlic cloves, crushed

14 oz/400 g canned plum
   tomatoes, chopped

2¾ oz/75 g chorizo sausage, sliced

1 green bell pepper, seeded and cut
   into strips

½ tsp paprika

¼ cup pitted black olives, halved

8 eggs

1 tbsp chopped fresh parsley

salt and pepper

crusty bread, to serve

VARIATION

Add a little spice to the dish by
incorporating 1 teaspoon chili
powder in step 4, if you like.

1 Cook the diced potatoes in a pan
of boiling water for 10 minutes,
or until softened. Drain thoroughly and
set aside.

2 Heat the olive oil in a large skillet.
Add the sliced onion and garlic
and cook gently for 2–3 minutes, until
the onion softens.

3 Add the chopped canned
tomatoes and cook over low heat
for about 10 minutes, until the mixture
has reduced slightly.

4 Stir the potatoes into the pan
with the chorizo, green bell
pepper, paprika, and olives. Season to
taste with salt and pepper. Cook for
5 minutes, stirring. Transfer to a
shallow ovenproof dish.

5 Make 8 small hollows in the top
of the mixture with the back of a
spoon and carefully break an egg into
each hollow. Season the eggs with salt
and pepper.

6 Cook in a preheated oven, 425°F/
220°C, for 5–6 minutes, or until
the eggs are just cooked.

7 Sprinkle the Spanish potatoes
with chopped parsley and serve
immediately with crusty bread.

potato, sausage & onion pie

serves four

1 lb 5 oz/600 g waxy potatoes,
    unpeeled and sliced

2 tbsp butter

4 thick pork and herb sausages

1 leek, sliced

2 garlic cloves, crushed

⅔ cup vegetable bouillon

⅔ cup hard cider or apple juice

2 tbsp chopped fresh sage

2 tbsp cornstarch

4 tbsp water

3/4 cup grated sharp cheese

salt and pepper

1 Cook the sliced potatoes in a pan of boiling water for 10 minutes. Drain and set aside.

2 Meanwhile, melt the butter in a skillet and cook the sausages for 8–10 minutes, turning them frequently so that they brown on all sides. Remove the sausages from the skillet and cut them into thick slices.

3 Add the leek, garlic, and sausage slices to the skillet and cook for 2–3 minutes.

4 Add the vegetable bouillon, hard cider or apple juice, and chopped sage. Season with salt and pepper. Blend the cornstarch with the water. Stir it into the skillet and bring to a boil, stirring until the sauce is thick and clear. Spoon the mixture into the base of a deep pie dish.

5 Layer the potato slices on top of the sausage mixture to cover it completely. Season with salt and pepper and sprinkle the grated cheese over the top.

6 Cook in a preheated oven, 375°F/190°C, for 25–30 minutes, or until the potatoes are cooked and the cheese is golden brown. Serve immediately, while the pie is hot.

tomato & sausage pan-fry

1 lb 5 oz/600 g potatoes, sliced

1 tbsp vegetable oil

8 flavored sausages

1 red onion, cut into 8 wedges

1 tbsp tomato paste

⅔ cup red wine

⅔ cup bottled strained tomatoes

2 large tomatoes, each cut into
   8 wedges

6 oz/175 g broccoli
   flowerets, blanched

2 tbsp chopped fresh basil

salt and pepper

shredded fresh basil, to garnish

1 Cook the sliced potatoes in a pan of boiling water for 7 minutes. Drain thoroughly and set aside.

2 Meanwhile, heat the oil in a large skillet. Add the sausages and cook for 5 minutes, turning them frequently to ensure that they are browned on all sides.

3 Add the onion wedges to the pan and continue to cook gently for 5 minutes more, stirring the mixture frequently.

4 Stir in the tomato paste, red wine, and the bottled strained tomatoes and mix well. Add the tomato wedges, broccoli flowerets, and chopped basil to the pan and mix carefully.

5 Add the parboiled potato slices to the pan. Cook the mixture for about 10 minutes, or until the sausages are completely cooked through. Season to taste with salt and pepper. Garnish with fresh shredded basil and serve hot.

veal italienne

serves four

5 tbsp butter

1 tbsp olive oil

1lb 8 oz/675 g potatoes, diced

4 veal scallops, 6 oz/175 g each

1 onion, cut into 8 wedges

2 garlic cloves, crushed

2 tbsp all-purpose flour

2 tbsp tomato paste

⅔ cup red wine

1¼ cups chicken bouillon

8 ripe tomatoes, skinned, seeded,
    and diced

¼ cup pitted black olives, halved

2 tbsp chopped fresh basil

salt and pepper

fresh basil leaves, to garnish

COOK'S TIP

For a quicker cooking time and
really tender meat, pound the
meat with a meat mallet to
flatten it slightly before cooking.

1 Heat the butter and oil in a large skillet. Add the diced potatoes and cook over medium heat, stirring frequently, for 5–7 minutes, until they begin to brown.

2 Remove the potatoes from the skillet with a slotted spoon and set aside.

3 Place the veal in the skillet and cook for 2–3 minutes on each side, until sealed. Remove from the skillet and then set aside.

4 Stir the onion and garlic into the skillet and cook for 2–3 minutes.

5 Add the flour and tomato paste and cook for 1 minute, stirring. Gradually blend in the red wine and chicken bouillon, stirring to make a smooth sauce.

6 Return the potatoes and veal to the skillet. Stir in the tomatoes, olives, and chopped basil and season with salt and pepper.

7 Transfer to a casserole and cook in a preheated oven, 350°F/ 180°C, for 1 hour, or until the potatoes and veal are cooked through. Garnish with fresh basil leaves and serve.

potato & broccoli pie

serves four

1 lb/450 g waxy potatoes, cut
    into chunks

2 tbsp butter

1 tbsp vegetable oil

6 oz/175 g lean pork, diced

1 red onion, cut into 8 wedges

2½ tbsp all-purpose flour, plus extra
    for dusting

⅔ cup vegetable bouillon

⅔ cup milk

2¾ oz/75 g dolcelatte
    cheese, crumbled

6 oz/75 g broccoli flowerets

¼ cup walnuts

8 oz/225 g ready-made puff pastry,
    thawed if frozen

milk, for glazing

salt and pepper

COOK'S TIP

Use a semihard, sharp cheese
instead of the dolcelatte,
if you like.

---

1 Cook the potato chunks in a pan of boiling water for 5 minutes. Drain and set aside.

2 Meanwhile, heat the butter and oil in a heavy pan. Add the pork and cook for 5 minutes, turning frequently, until browned.

3 Add the onion and cook for 2 minutes more. Stir in the flour and cook for 1 minute, then gradually stir in the vegetable bouillon and milk. Bring to a boil, stirring constantly.

4 Add the dolcelatte, broccoli flowerets, potatoes, and walnuts to the pan and simmer for 5 minutes. Season with salt and pepper to taste, then spoon the mixture into a pie dish.

5 On a floured counter, roll out the pastry until 1-inch/2.5-cm larger than the dish. Cut a 1-inch/2.5-cm wide strip from the pastry. Dampen the edge of the dish and place the pastry strip around it. Brush with milk and put the pastry lid on top.

6 Seal and crimp the edges and make 2 small slits in the center of the lid. Brush with milk and cook in a preheated oven, 400°F/200°C, for 25 minutes, or until the pastry has risen and is golden.

strained dhal with meatballs

serves six

1½ cups masoor dhal

1 tsp crushed fresh gingerroot

1 tsp crushed garlic

½ tsp ground turmeric

1½ tsp chili powder

1½ tsp salt

3 tbsp lemon juice

3½ cups water

1 lb/450 g canned meatballs

TO GARNISH

3 fresh green chiles, seeded and
    chopped finely

fresh cilantro leaves, chopped

BAGHAAR

⅔ cup vegetable oil

3 garlic cloves

4 dried red chiles

1 tsp white cumin seeds

POTATO FRIES

pinch of salt

1 lb/450 g potatoes, sliced thinly

1¼ cups vegetable oil

1 Rinse the lentils, and pick over
them to remove any stones.

2 Place the lentils in a pan and
cover with 2½ cups water. Add
the ginger, garlic, turmeric, and chili
powder, bring to a boil, and cook until
the lentils are soft and mushy. Add the
salt, stirring.

3 Mash the lentils, then push them
through a strainer, reserving the
liquid. Add the lemon juice to the
strained liquid.

4 Stir 1¼ cups of the water into the
strained liquid and bring to a boil
over low heat. Drops the meatballs
gently into the lentil mixture. Set aside.

5 Prepare the baghaar. Heat the oil
in a pan. Add the garlic, dried red
chiles, and white cumin seeds and
cook for 2 minutes. Pour the baghaar
over the lentil mixture, stirring to mix.

6 For the potato fries, rub the salt
over the potato slices. Heat the oil
in a skillet and fry the potatoes,
turning, until crisp. Garnish the
meatballs with the potato fries, chiles,
and cilantro.

quick baked chicken

serves four

1 lb 2 oz/500 g ground chicken
1 large onion, chopped finely
2 carrots, chopped finely
2 tbsp all-purpose flour
1 tbsp tomato paste
1¼ cups chicken bouillon
pinch of fresh thyme
generous 3½ cups mashed
    potatoes, creamed with butter
    and milk and well seasoned
¾ cup grated semihard white cheese
salt and pepper
cooked peas, to serve

1 Brown the ground chicken, onion, and carrots in a nonstick pan for 5 minutes, stirring frequently.

2 Sprinkle the chicken with the flour and cook over low heat for 2 minutes more.

3 Gradually blend in the tomato paste and chicken bouillon, then simmer for 15 minutes. Season to taste with salt and pepper and add a pinch of fresh thyme.

4 Using a slotted spoon, transfer the chicken and vegetable mixture to a casserole and let cool.

5 Spoon the mashed potato over the chicken mixture and sprinkle with cheese. Bake in a preheated oven, 400°F/200°C, for 20 minutes, or until the cheese is bubbling and golden, then serve, straight from the casserole, with the peas.

potato crisp pie

serves four

1 lb 5 oz/600 g waxy
    potatoes, sliced

5 tbsp butter

1 skinless, boneless chicken breast
    portion, about 6 oz/175 g

2 garlic cloves, crushed

4 scallions, sliced

2½ tbsp all-purpose flour

⅔ cup dry white wine

⅔ cup heavy cream

8 oz/225 g broccoli flowerets

4 large tomatoes, sliced

2¾ oz/75 g Swiss cheese, sliced

1 cup plain yogurt

⅓ cup rolled oats, toasted

1 Cook the potatoes in a pan of boiling water for 10 minutes. Drain and set aside.

2 Meanwhile, melt the butter in a skillet. Cut the chicken into strips and cook for 5 minutes, turning. Add the garlic and scallions and cook for 2 minutes more.

3 Stir in the flour and cook for 1 minute. Gradually add the wine and cream. Bring to a boil, stirring, then reduce the heat until the sauce is simmering, and cook for 5 minutes.

4 Meanwhile, blanch the broccoli in boiling water. Drain and refresh in cold water.

5 Place half of the potatoes in the base of a pie dish and top with half of the tomatoes and half of the broccoli flowerets.

6 Spoon the chicken sauce on top and repeat the layers in the same order once more.

7 Arrange the slices of Swiss cheese on top of the layers and spoon over the yogurt. Sprinkle with the rolled oats and cook in a preheated oven, 400°F/200°C, for 25 minutes, until the top is golden brown. Serve the pie immediately.

gardener's chicken

serves four

4 cups parsnips, peeled
and chopped

2 small carrots, peeled and chopped

½ cup fresh bread crumbs

¼ tsp grated nutmeg

1 tbsp chopped fresh parsley, plus
extra to garnish

3 lb 5 oz/1.5 kg chicken

bunch of fresh parsley

½ onion, cut into wedges

2 tbsp butter, softened

4 tbsp olive oil

1 lb 2 oz/500 g new
potatoes, scrubbed

1 lb 2 oz/500 g baby carrots,
washed and trimmed

salt and pepper

COOK'S TIP

The quickest way to make ½ cup
fresh bread crumbs is to cut the
crusts off 1 thick or 2 thin slices
of bread and process in a food
processor for a few seconds. This
produces more even-size
crumbs than grating and spares
the knuckles.

1 To make the stuffing, put the parsnips and carrots into a pan. Cover with water and bring to a boil. Cover the pan and simmer until tender. Drain well, then process in a blender or food processor. Transfer the purée to a bowl and let cool.

2 Mix in the bread crumbs, nutmeg, and chopped parsley and season to taste with salt and pepper.

3 Put the stuffing into the neck end of the chicken and push a little of the stuffing under the skin over the breast meat. Secure the flap of skin with a small metal skewer or toothpick.

4 Place the bunch of parsley and onion inside the cavity of the chicken, then place the chicken in a large roasting pan.

5 Spread the butter over the skin and season with salt and pepper. Cover with aluminum foil and place in a preheated oven, 375°F/190°C, for 30 minutes.

6 Meanwhile, heat the oil in a skillet, and brown the potatoes.

7 Transfer the potatoes to the roasting pan and add the baby carrots. Baste the chicken and continue to cook for 1 hour more, basting the chicken and vegetables after 30 minutes. Remove the foil for the last 20 minutes to let the skin crisp. Garnish the vegetables with chopped parsley and serve.

chicken & potato casserole

serves four

2 tbsp vegetable oil

¼ cup butter

4 chicken portions, about 8 oz/
  225 g each

2 leeks, sliced

1 garlic clove, crushed

4 tbsp all-purpose flour

3¾ cups chicken bouillon

1¼ cups dry white wine

4½ oz/125 g baby carrots,
  halved lengthwise

4½ oz/125 g baby corn,
  halved lengthwise

1 lb/450 g small new potatoes

1 bouquet garni

⅔ cup heavy cream

salt and pepper

rice or broccoli, to serve

1 Heat the oil and butter in a large skillet. Cook the chicken for 10 minutes, turning until browned all over. Transfer the chicken to a casserole using a slotted spoon.

2 Add the leeks and garlic to the skillet and cook for 2–3 minutes, stirring. Stir in the flour and cook for another minute. Remove the skillet from the heat and stir in the chicken bouillon and wine. Season well.

3 Return the skillet to the heat and bring the mixture to a boil. Stir in the carrots, corn, potatoes, and bouquet garni.

4 Transfer the mixture to the casserole. Cover and cook in a preheated oven, 350°F/180°C, for about 1 hour.

5 Remove the casserole from the oven and stir in the cream. Return the casserole to the oven, uncovered, and cook for 15 minutes more. Remove the bouquet garni and discard. Taste and adjust the seasoning, if necessary. Serve with plain rice or fresh vegetables.

chicken & banana cakes

serves four

2⅔ cups diced mealy potatoes

8 oz/225 g ground chicken

1 large banana

2 tbsp all-purpose flour

1 tsp lemon juice

1 onion, chopped finely

2 tbsp chopped fresh sage

2 tbsp butter

2 tbsp vegetable oil

⅔ cup light cream

⅔ cup chicken bouillon

salt and pepper

fresh sage leaves, to garnish

1 Cook the diced potatoes in a pan of boiling water for 10 minutes, until cooked through. Drain and mash the potatoes until they are smooth. Stir in the chicken.

2 Mash the banana and add it to the potatoes with the flour, lemon juice, onion, and half of the chopped sage. Season to taste with salt and pepper and stir the mixture together.

3 Divide the mixture into 8 equal portions. With lightly floured hands, shape each portion into a round patty.

4 Heat the butter and oil in a skillet. Add the potato cakes and cook for 12–15 minutes, or until cooked through, turning once. Remove from the skillet and keep warm.

5 Stir in the cream and bouillon with the remaining sage. Cook gently over low heat for 2–3 minutes.

6 Arrange the potato cakes on a serving plate. Garnish with fresh sage leaves and serve with the cream and sage sauce.

potato, leek & chicken pie

serves four

225 g/8 oz waxy potatoes, diced

5 tbsp butter

1 skinless, boneless chicken breast
portion, about 6 oz/175 g, diced

1 leek, sliced

5½ oz/150 g crimini mushrooms,
sliced

2½ tbsp all-purpose flour

1¼ cups milk

1 tbsp Dijon mustard

2 tbsp chopped fresh sage

8 oz/225 g phyllo pastry, thawed
if frozen

3 tbsp butter, melted

salt and pepper

1 Cook the diced potatoes in a pan
of boiling water for 5 minutes.
Drain and set aside.

2 Melt the butter in a skillet and
cook the chicken for 5 minutes, or
until browned all over.

3 Add the leek and mushrooms and
cook over medium heat, stirring
occasionally, for 3 minutes. Stir in the
flour and cook, stirring constantly, for 1
minute. Gradually add the milk and
bring to a boil. Add the mustard,
chopped sage, and potatoes, then
simmer the mixture for 10 minutes.

4 Meanwhile, line a deep pie dish
with half of the sheets of phyllo
pastry. Spoon the sauce into the dish
and cover with one sheet of pastry.
Brush the pastry with butter and lay
another sheet on top. Brush this sheet
with butter.

5 Cut the remaining phyllo pastry
into strips and fold them onto the
top of the pie to create an attractive,
ruffled effect. Brush the strips with the
remaining melted butter and cook in a
preheated oven, 350°F/180°C, for
45 minutes, or until golden brown and
crisp. Serve hot.

COOK'S TIP

If the top of the pie starts
to brown too quickly, cover it
with foil halfway through the
cooking time to let the pastry
base cook through without
the top burning.

chicken & potato bake

2 tbsp olive oil

4 lean skinless, boneless chicken
breast portions

1 bunch of scallions, chopped

12 oz/350 g young spring carrots,
scrubbed and sliced

4½ oz/125 g green beans, trimmed
and sliced

2½ cups chicken bouillon

12 oz/350 g small new
potatoes, scrubbed

1 small bunch of mixed fresh herbs,
such as thyme, rosemary, bay,
and parsley

2 tbsp cornstarch

2–3 tbsp cold water

salt and pepper

fresh mixed herb sprigs,
to garnish

2 Add the scallions, carrots, and green beans and cook over low heat for 3–4 minutes.

3 Return the chicken to the casserole and add the bouillon with the potatoes and herbs. Season with salt and pepper, bring to a boil, then cover the casserole and transfer to the oven. Bake in a preheated oven, 375°F/190°C, for 40–50 minutes, until the potatoes are tender.

1 Heat the oil in a large flameproof casserole and add the chicken. Cook gently for 5–8 minutes, until well browned on both sides. Remove from the casserole with a slotted spoon and set aside.

4 Blend the cornstarch with the cold water to a smooth paste. Add to the casserole, stirring constantly until thickened. Cover and cook for 5 minutes more. Garnish with fresh herbs and serve immediately.

potato & turkey pie

serves four

1²⁄₃ cup waxy potatoes, diced

2 tbsp butter

1 tbsp vegetable oil

10½ oz/300 g lean turkey
    meat, diced

1 red onion, halved and sliced

2 tbsp all-purpose flour, plus extra
    for dusting

1¼ cups milk

²⁄₃ cup heavy cream

2 celery stalks, sliced

⅓ cup dried apricots, chopped

¼ cup walnut pieces

2 tbsp chopped fresh parsley

8 oz/225 g ready-made
    unsweetened shortcrust pastry,
    thawed if frozen

beaten egg, for brushing

salt and pepper

1 Cook the diced potatoes in a pan of boiling water for 10 minutes, until tender. Drain and set aside.

2 Meanwhile, heat the butter and oil in a heavy pan. Add the diced turkey and cook over medium heat, stirring frequently, for 5 minutes, until golden brown.

3 Add the sliced onion and cook for 2–3 minutes. Stir in the flour and cook, stirring constantly, for 1 minute. Gradually stir in the milk and cream. Bring to a boil, stirring, then lower the heat to a simmer.

4 Stir in the celery, apricots, walnut pieces, parsley, and potatoes. Season well with salt and pepper. Spoon the potato and turkey mixture into the base of a 5-cup pie dish.

5 On a lightly floured counter, roll out the pastry to 1-inch/2.5-cm larger than the dish. Trim a 1-inch/2.5-cm wide strip and place it on the dampened rim of the dish. Brush with water and cover with the pastry lid.

6 Brush the top of the pie with beaten egg to glaze and cook in a preheated oven, 400°F/200°C, for 25–30 minutes, or until the pie is cooked and golden brown. Serve the pie immediately.

Fish

There is no denying that fish and potatoes are a terrific combination. In these recipes, potatoes are used in a variety of ways to enhance the fish. They are used to form a crispy coating for cod, and mashed to make the basis of fishcakes and fritters. They are sliced to form part of a layered pie, and sautéed with shallots to create the perfect accompaniment to a red mullet wrapped in prosciutto. For health-conscious cooks, the nutritious value of these dishes is unbeatable.

salt cod fritters

serves six

1 lb/450 g salt cod

12 oz/350 g mealy baking potatoes

olive oil, for deep-frying

1 onion, very finely chopped

1 garlic clove, crushed

4 tbsp very finely chopped fresh
parsley or cilantro

1 tbsp capers in brine, drained and
chopped finely, (optional)

1 medium egg, lightly beaten

salt and pepper

chopped fresh parsley, to garnish

aïoli, to serve

1 Break the salt cod into pieces and
place in a bowl. Add enough
water to cover and let stand for
48 hours, changing the water 4 times.

2 Drain the salt cod, then cook in
boiling water for 20–25 minutes,
until tender. Drain, then remove all the
skin and bones. Using a fork, flake the
fish into fine pieces that still retain
some texture.

3 Meanwhile, boil the potatoes in
their skins until tender. Drain, peel,
then mash in a large bowl. Set aside.

4 Heat 1 tablespoon of oil in a
skillet. Add the onion and garlic
and cook for 5 minutes, stirring
frequently, until tender but not brown.
Remove with a slotted spoon and drain
on paper towels.

5 Stir the salt cod, onion, and garlic
into the mashed potatoes. Stir in
the parsley or cilantro, and the capers if
using. Season generously with pepper.

6 Stir in the beaten egg. Cover
with plastic wrap and chill for
30 minutes, then adjust the seasoning.

7 Heat 2 inch/5 cm oil in a skillet to
350–375°F/180–190°C or until a
cube of bread browns in 30 seconds.
Drop tablespoonfuls of the salt cod
mixture into the hot oil and cook for
about 8 minutes, or until golden brown
and set. Do not fry more than 6 at a
time because the oil will become too
cold and the fritters will become soggy.
You will get 18–20 fritters.

8 Drain the fritters on paper towels.
Serve immediately, garnished
with the parsley, with aïoli for dipping.

tuna & cheese quiche

serves four

SHELL

2 ⅔ cups diced mealy potatoes

2 tbsp butter

6 tbsp all-purpose flour, plus extra
for dusting

mixed vegetables or salad, to serve

FILLING

1 tbsp vegetable oil

1 shallot, chopped

1 garlic clove, crushed

1 red bell pepper, seeded and diced

6 oz/175g canned tuna in
brine, drained

scant ⅓ cup canned corn, drained

⅔ cup skim milk

3 eggs, beaten

1 tbsp chopped fresh dill

½ cup grated sharp low-
fat cheese

salt and pepper

TO GARNISH

fresh dill sprigs

lemon wedges

1 Cook the potatoes in a pan of
boiling water for 10 minutes,
or until tender.

2 Drain and mash the potatoes.
Add the butter and flour and mix
to form a dough.

3 Knead the potato dough on a
floured counter and press the
mixture into a 8-inch /20-cm flan pan.
Prick the base with a fork. Line with
baking parchment and baking beans
and bake blind in a preheated oven,
400°F/200°C, for 20 minutes.

4 Heat the oil in a skillet. Cook the
shallot, garlic, and bell pepper for
5 minutes. Spoon the mixture into the
flan shell. Flake the tuna and arrange it
on top with the corn.

5 In a bowl, combine the milk,
eggs, and dill and season.

6 Pour the egg and dill mixture into
the flan shell and sprinkle the
grated cheese on top.

7 Bake in the oven for 20 minutes,
or until the filling has set. Garnish
the flan with fresh dill and lemon
wedges. Serve with mixed vegetables
or salad.

cod & fries

1 lb 8 oz/675 g potatoes

4 pieces cod fillet

oil for deep frying

BATTER:

i oz/15 g fresh yeast

1¼ cups beer

2 cups all-purpose flour

2 tsp salt

MAYONNAISE

1 egg yolk

1 tsp whole-grain mustard

1 tbsp lemon juice

1 cup light olive oil

salt and pepper

1 For the batter, cream the yeast with a little of the beer to a smooth paste. Gradually stir in the rest of the beer. Sift the all-purpose flour and salt into a bowl, make a well in the center, and add the yeast mixture. Gradually whisk to a smooth batter. Cover and leave at room temperature for 1 hour.

2 For the mayonnaise, put the egg yolk, mustard, lemon juice, and seasoning into a food processor. Process for 30 seconds, until frothy.

Begin adding the olive oil, drop by drop, until the mixture begins to thicken. Continue adding the oil in a slow, steady stream until all the oil has been incorporated. Taste for seasoning. Thin with a little hot water if the mayonnaise is too thick. Chill the mayonnaise until needed.

3 For the fish and fries, cut the potatoes into fries about ½-inch/ 1.5-cm thick. Heat a large pan half-filled with vegetable oil to 275°F/ 140°C or until a cube of bread browns in 1 minute. Cook the fries, in batches, for about 5 minutes, until they are cooked through but not browned. Place the fries to drain on paper towels and set aside.

4 Increase the heat to 325°F/160°C or until a cube of bread browns in 45 seconds. Season the fish, then dip into the batter. Fry 2 pieces at a time

for 7–8 minutes, until deep golden brown and cooked through. Drain thoroughly on paper towels and keep warm while you cook remaining fish. Keep these warm while you finish cooking the fries.

5 Increase the heat to 375°F/190°C or until a cube of bread browns in 30 seconds. Fry the fries again, in batches, for 2–3 minutes, until crisp and golden. Drain on paper towels and sprinkle with salt.

6 Serve the fish with the fries and mayonnaise, garnished with lemon wedges and parsley sprigs.

soused trout & potato salad

serves four

4 trout, about 8–12 oz/225–350 g
   each, filleted

1 onion, very thinly sliced

2 bay leaves

fresh parsley and dill sprigs, or other
   fresh herbs

10–12 black peppercorns

4–6 cloves

⅔ cup red wine vinegar

salt

salad greens, to garnish

POTATO SALAD

1 lb 2 oz/500g small
   new potatoes

2 tbsp French dressing

4 tbsp thick low-fat mayonnaise

3–4 scallions, sliced

1 Trim the trout fillets, cutting off any pieces of fin. If you like, remove the skin—use a sharp knife and, beginning at the tail end, carefully cut the flesh from the skin, pressing the knife down firmly as you go.

2 Lightly grease a shallow ovenproof dish and lay the fillets in it, packing them fairly tightly together but keeping them in a single layer. Arrange the sliced onion, bay leaves, and herbs over the fish.

3 Put the peppercorns, cloves, salt, and vinegar into a pan and bring almost to a boil. Remove from the heat and pour evenly over the fish. Leave to cool, then cover, and marinate in the refrigerator for 24 hours.

4 Cover the dish with foil and cook in a preheated oven, 325°F/ 160°C for 15 minutes. Leave until cold and then cover, and chill thoroughly.

5 Cook the potatoes in boiling salted water for 10–15 minutes, until just tender. Drain. While still warm, cut into large dice and place in a bowl. Combine the French dressing and mayonnaise, add to the potatoes while warm, and toss evenly. Leave until cold, then sprinkle the potato salad with chopped scallions.

6 Place the fish on serving plates and pour a little of the juices over each portion of fish. Garnish with salad greens and serve immediately with the potato salad.

layered fish & potato pie

serves four

2 lb/900 g waxy potatoes, sliced

5 tbsp butter

1 red onion, halved and sliced

⅓ cup all-purpose flour

2 cups milk

⅔ cup heavy cream

8 oz/225 g smoked haddock
   fillet, skinned and diced

8 oz/225 g cod fillet, skinned and
   diced

1 red bell pepper, seeded and diced

4½ oz/125 g broccoli flowerets

scant ⅔ cup freshly grated
   Parmesan cheese

salt and pepper

1 Cook the sliced potatoes in a pan of boiling water for 10 minutes. Drain and set aside.

2 Meanwhile, melt the butter in a pan, then add the onion, and cook gently for 3–4 minutes.

3 Add the flour and cook for 1 minute. Blend in the milk and cream and bring to a boil, stirring until the sauce has thickened.

4 Arrange about half of the potato slices in the base of a shallow, ovenproof dish.

5 Add the fish, diced bell pepper, and broccoli to the sauce and cook over low heat for 10 minutes. Season with salt and pepper, then spoon the mixture over the potatoes in the dish.

6 Arrange the remaining potato slices in a layer over the fish mixture. Sprinkle the Parmesan cheese over the top.

7 Cook in a preheated oven, 350°F/ 180°C, for 30 minutes, or until the the topping is golden.

fish balls with tomato sauce

serves four

2⅔ cups diced mealy potatoes

8 oz/225 g smoked fish fillet, such
as cod, skinned

3 tbsp butter

2 eggs, beaten

1 tbsp chopped fresh dill

½ tsp cayenne pepper

vegetable oil, for deep-frying

salt and pepper

fresh dill sprigs, to garnish

SAUCE

1¼ cups bottled strained tomatoes

1 tbsp tomato paste

2 tbsp chopped fresh dill

⅔ cup fish bouillon

1 Cook the diced potatoes in a pan
of boiling water for 10 minutes,
or until tender. Drain thoroughly, then
add the butter to the potato and mash
until smooth. Season to taste with salt
and pepper.

2 Meanwhile, poach the fish in
boiling water for 10 minutes,
turning once. Drain and mash the fish.
Stir it into the potatoes and let cool.

3 While the potato and fish mixture
is cooling, make the sauce. Put
the bottled strained tomatoes, tomato
paste, dill, and bouillon in a pan and
bring to a boil. Reduce the heat, then
cover the pan, and simmer for about
20 minutes, until thickened.

4 Add the eggs, dill, and cayenne
pepper to the potato and fish
mixture and beat until well mixed.

5 In a large pan, heat the oil to
350–375°F/180–190°C, or until
a cube of bread browns in 30 seconds.
Drop dessertspoons of the potato
mixture into the oil and cook for
3–4 minutes, until golden brown.
Remove with a slotted spoon and drain
on paper towels.

6 Garnish the potato and fish balls
with fresh dill sprigs and serve
with the tomato sauce.

smoked fish pie

2 tbsp olive oil

1 onion, chopped finely

1 leek, sliced thinly

1 carrot, diced

1 celery stalk, diced

½ cup white mushrooms, halved

grated rind 1 lemon

12 oz/350 g skinless smoked cod or
   haddock fillet, diced

12 oz/375 g skinless white fish fillet,
   such as haddock, hake, or
   monkfish, diced

8 oz/225 g cooked peeled shrimp

2 tbsp chopped fresh parsley

1 tbsp chopped fresh dill

salt and pepper

dill sprigs, to garnish

fresh cooked vegetables, to serve

SAUCE

4 tbsp butter

4 tbsp all-purpose flour

1 tsp mustard powder

2½ cups milk

generous ¾ cup grated Swiss cheese

TOPPING

1lb 8 oz/675 g potatoes, unpeeled

4 tbsp butter, melted

¼ cup grated Swiss cheese

salt

1 For the sauce, heat the butter in a large pan and when melted, add the flour and mustard powder. Stir until smooth and cook over very low heat for 2 minutes without coloring. Gradually whisk in the milk until smooth. Simmer gently for 2 minutes, then stir in the cheese until smooth. Remove from the heat and put some plastic wrap over the surface of the sauce to prevent a skin from forming. Set aside.

2 Meanwhile, for the topping, boil the whole potatoes in plenty of lightly salted water for 15 minutes. Drain well and let stand until cool enough to handle.

3 Heat the olive oil in a clean pan and add the onion. Cook over medium heat, stirring occasionally, for 5 minutes, until softened. Add the leek, carrot, celery, and mushrooms, and cook for 10 minutes more, until the vegetables have softened. Stir in the lemon rind and cook briefly.

4 Add the softened vegetables to the sauce with the fish, shrimp, parsley, and dill. Season to taste with salt and pepper and transfer to a greased 7½-cup casserole.

5 Peel the cooled potatoes and grate them coarsely. Combine with the melted butter. Cover the filling evenly with the grated potato and sprinkle with the grated Swiss cheese.

6 Cover the pie loosely with aluminum foil and bake in a preheated oven, 400°F/200°C, for 30 minutes. Remove the foil and bake for about 30 minutes more, until the topping is tender and golden and the filling is bubbling and cooked through. Garnish and serve immediately with your favorite selection of vegetables.

fish turnovers

serves four

DOUGH

4 cups self-rising flour, plus extra
for dusting

pinch of salt

1¼ cups butter, diced, plus extra
for greasing

1 egg, lightly beaten

FILLING

¼ cup butter

1 small leek, diced

1 small onion, chopped finely

1 carrot, diced

1½ cups potatoes, diced

12 oz/350 g firm white fish fillet, cut
into 1-inch/2.5-cm pieces

4 tsp white wine vinegar

¼ cup grated Cheddar cheese

1 tsp chopped fresh tarragon

salt and pepper

TO SERVE

mixed salad greens and tomatoes

1 In a large bowl, sift together the flour and salt. Add the butter and rub it in with your fingertips until the mixture resembles coarse bread crumbs. Add about 3 tablespoons cold water and bring together to form a dough. Knead briefly until smooth. Wrap in plastic wrap and chill in the refrigerator for 30 minutes.

2 Meanwhile, to make the filling, melt half the butter in a large skillet and add the leek, onion, and carrot. Cook over low heat, stirring occasionally, for 7–8 minutes, until the vegetables are softened. Remove the skillet from the heat, put to one side, and leave the mixture to cool slightly.

3 Put the vegetable mixture into a large mixing bowl and add the potatoes, fish, vinegar, remaining butter, cheese, tarragon, and seasoning. Set aside.

4 Remove the pastry from the refrigerator and roll out thinly on a lightly floured surface. Using a pastry cutter, press out 4 x 7½-inch/19-cm circles. Alternatively, use a small plate of a similar size as a template and cut around it with a sharp knife. Divide the filling among the 4 circles. Moisten the edges of the pastry and fold over. Pinch to seal. Crimp the edges firmly and place the turnovers on a lightly greased cookie sheet. Brush them generously with the beaten egg to glaze, avoiding the base of the pastry to prevent the turnovers from sticking to the cookie sheet.

5 Bake the turnovers in a preheated oven, 400°F/200°C, for 15 minutes. Remove from the oven and brush again with the egg glaze. Return to the oven for 20 minutes more. Serve the turnovers hot or cold with mixed greens and tomatoes.

ocean pie

serves four

1 lb 2 oz/500 g cod or haddock
   fillet, skinned

8 oz/225 g salmon steak

scant 2 cups skim milk

1 bay leaf

2 lb 4 oz/1 kg potatoes

½ cup peeled shrimp, thawed
   if frozen

¼ cup butter or margarine

4 tbsp all-purpose flour

2–4 tbsp white wine

1 tsp chopped fresh dill or ½ tsp
   dried dill

2 tbsp drained capers

salt and pepper

few whole shrimp in their shells,
   to garnish

VARIATION

Substitute fresh scallops for the
shrimp in the pie. Sear them
briefly in hot oil for 1–2 minutes
before adding them to the filling
in step 3. Cut them in half first if
they are large.

1 Put the fish into a pan with
1¼ cups of the milk, the bay leaf,
and seasoning to taste. Bring to a boil,
cover, and simmer gently for about
10–15 minutes, until tender.

2 Coarsely chop the potatoes and
cook in lightly salted, boiling
water until tender.

3 Drain the fish, reserving the
cooking liquid. Measure the
cooking liquid and make up to 1¼ cups
with more milk if necessary. Flake the
fish, discarding any bones and place in
a shallow ovenproof dish. Gently stir in
the shrimp.

4 Melt half the butter or margarine
in a pan, add the flour and cook,
stirring constantly, for a minute or so.
Gradually stir in the reserved cooking
liquor and the wine and bring to a boil.
Add the dill, capers, and seasoning to
taste and simmer until thickened. Pour
over the fish and mix well.

5 Drain the potatoes and mash well
with a fork or potato masher,
adding the remaining butter or
margarine, seasoning, and sufficient
milk to give a piping consistency.

6 Put the mashed potato into
a pastry bag. Use a large star tip
and pipe over the fish. Cook in a
preheated oven, 400°F/200°C. for
about 25 minutes. until piping hot and
browned. Serve the pie immediately
garnished with the whole shrimp.

poached trout

serves four

3 lb/1.3 kg trout, filleted

1 lb 9 oz/700 g new potatoes

3 scallions, chopped finely

1 egg, hard-cooked and chopped

salad greens, to serve

COURT-BOUILLON

3½ cups cold water

3½ cups dry white wine

3 tbsp white wine vinegar

2 large carrots, chopped coarsely

1 onion, chopped coarsely

2 celery stalks, chopped coarsely

2 leeks, chopped coarsely

2 garlic cloves, chopped coarsely

2 fresh bay leaves

4 fresh parsley sprigs

4 fresh thyme sprigs

6 black peppercorns

1 tsp salt

WATERCRESS MAYONNAISE

1 egg yolk

1 tsp Dijon mustard

1 tsp white wine vinegar

1¾ oz/50 g watercress
   leaves, chopped

1 cup light olive oil

salt and pepper

1 First make the court-bouillon. Place all the ingredients in a large pan and gradually bring to a boil. Cover and simmer gently for about 30 minutes. Strain the liquid through a fine strainer into a clean pan. Bring to a boil again and simmer rapidly, uncovered, for 15–20 minutes, until the court-bouillon is reduced to 2½ cups.

2 Place the trout in a large skillet or pan. Add the court-bouillon and gradually bring to a boil. Remove from the heat and leave the fish in the poaching liquid to go cold.

3 Meanwhile, make the watercress mayonnaise. Put the egg yolk, mustard, wine vinegar, watercress, and seasoning into a food processor or blender and process for 30 seconds, until foaming. Begin adding the olive oil, drop by drop, until the mixture begins to thicken. Continue adding the oil in a slow steady stream until it is all incorporated. Add a little hot water if the mixture seems too thick. Season to taste and set aside.

4 Cook the potatoes in lightly salted, boiling water for 12–15 minutes, until tender. Drain well and refresh them under cold running water. Set the potatoes aside until cold.

5 When the potatoes are cold, cut them in half if they are very large, and toss thoroughly with the watercress mayonnaise, finely chopped scallions, and hard-cooked egg.

6 Remove the fish from the poaching liquid and drain on paper towels. Carefully pull the skin away from each of the trout and discard. Serve with the potato salad and salad greens.

214

herring & potato pie

serves four

1 tbsp Dijon mustard

½ cup butter, softened

1 lb/450 g herring fillets

1 lb 10 oz/750 g potatoes

1 large onion, sliced

2 cooking apples, sliced thinly

1 tsp chopped fresh sage

2½ cups hot fish bouillon

1 cup crustless Italian-style
 bread crumbs

salt and pepper

fresh parsley sprigs, to garnish

VARIATION

If herrings are unavailable,
substitute mackerel or sardines.

1 Mix the mustard with a fourth of the butter until smooth. Spread this mixture over the cut sides of the herring fillets. Season and roll up the fillets. Set aside. Generously grease an 8-cup pie pan with some of the remaining butter.

2 Thinly slice the potatoes, using a mandoline if possible. Blanch for 3 minutes in plenty of lightly salted, boiling, water until just tender. Drain well, then refresh under cold water and pat dry.

3 Heat a third of the remaining butter in a skillet and add the onion. Cook gently for 8–10 minutes, until softened but not colored. Remove from the heat and set aside.

4 Put half the potato slices into the base of the pie dish with some seasoning, then add half the apples and half the onion. Put the herring fillets on top and sprinkle with the sage. Repeat the layers in reverse order, ending with potato. Season and add enough hot bouillon to come halfway up the sides of the dish.

5 Melt the remaining butter and stir in the bread crumbs until well combined. Sprinkle the bread crumbs over the pie. Bake in a preheated oven, 375°F/190°C, for 40–50 minutes until the bread crumbs are golden and the herrings are cooked through. Serve garnished with parsley.

Vegetarian

The potato has become a valued staple of the vegetarian diet, yet anyone who thought this would make for dull eating will be pleasantly surprised by the rich variety of dishes in this chapter. In addition to traditional, hearty baked dishes, there are also influences from around the world in dishes such as Bean Curd & Vegetable Stir-fry from China, and Potato & Cauliflower Curry from India. They all make exciting eating at any time of year.

potato-topped vegetables

1 carrot, diced

6 oz/175 g cauliflower flowerets

6 oz/175 g broccoli flowerets

1 fennel bulb, sliced

2¾ oz/75 g green beans, halved

2 tbsp butter

¼ cup all-purpose flour

⅔ cup vegetable bouillon

⅔ cup dry white wine

⅔ cup milk

6 oz/175 g crimini mushrooms, cut
    into quarters

2 tbsp chopped fresh sage

TOPPING

generous 5 cups diced
    mealy potatoes

2 tbsp butter

4 tbsp plain yogurt

1 cup freshly grated Parmesan cheese

1 tsp fennel seeds

salt and pepper

1 Cook the carrot, cauliflower, broccoli, fennel, and beans in a large pan of boiling water for 10 minutes, until just tender. Drain the vegetables thoroughly and set aside.

2 Melt the butter in a pan. Stir in the flour and cook for 1 minute. Remove from the heat and stir in the bouillon, wine, and milk. Return to the heat and bring to a boil, stirring until thickened. Stir in the reserved vegetables, mushrooms, and sage.

3 Meanwhile, make the topping. Cook the diced potatoes in a pan of boiling water for 10–15 minutes. Drain and mash with the butter, yogurt, and half the Parmesan cheese. Stir in the fennel seeds.

4 Spoon the vegetable mixture into a 4-cup pie dish. Spoon the

potato over the top and sprinkle with the remaining cheese. Cook in a preheated oven, 375°F/190°C, for 30–35 minutes, until golden.

three cheese soufflé

serves four

2 tbsp butter

2 tsp all-purpose flour

2 lb/900 g mealy potatoes

8 eggs, separated

¼ cup grated Swiss cheese

¼ cup crumbled blue cheese

¼ cup grated sharp cheese

salt and pepper

1 Butter a 10-cup soufflé dish and dust with the flour. Set aside.

2 Cook the potatoes in a pan of boiling water until tender. Mash until very smooth and then transfer to a mixing bowl to cool.

3 Beat the egg yolks into the potato and stir in all three of the cheeses with the salt and pepper. Stir lightly until the cheeses are well combined.

4 Whisk the egg whites until standing in peaks, then gently fold them into the potato mixture with a metal spoon until fully incorporated.

5 Spoon the potato mixture into the prepared soufflé dish.

6 Cook in a preheated oven, 425°F/ 220°C, for 35–40 minutes, until risen and set. Serve immediately.

layered cheese & potatoes

serves four

2 lb/900 g unpeeled waxy potatoes,
  cut into wedges

2 tbsp butter

1 red onion, halved and sliced

2 garlic cloves, crushed

¼ cup all-purpose flour

2½ cups milk

14 oz/400 g canned artichoke
  hearts in brine, drained
  and halved

5½ oz/150 g frozen mixed
  vegetables, thawed

1¼ cups grated Swiss cheese

1¼ cups grated sharp cheese

½ cup crumbled Gorgonzola

⅓ cup freshly grated
  Parmesan cheese

8 oz/225 g firm bean curd, drained
  and sliced

2 tbsp chopped fresh thyme

salt and pepper

fresh thyme sprigs, to garnish

VARIATION

If you find the flavor of
Gorgonzola too powerful, you
could substitute the milder-
flavored Docelatte.

---

1 Cook the potato wedges in a pan of boiling water for 10 minutes. Drain thoroughly.

2 Meanwhile, melt the butter in a pan. Add the sliced onion and garlic and cook over low heat, stirring frequently, for 2–3 minutes.

3 Stir the flour into the pan and cook, stirring, for 1 minute. Gradually add the milk and bring to a boil, stirring constantly.

4 Reduce the heat and add the artichoke hearts, mixed vegetables, half of each of the 4 cheeses, and the bean curd to the pan, mixing well. Stir in the chopped thyme and season with salt and pepper to taste.

5 Arrange a layer of parboiled potato wedges in the base of a shallow ovenproof dish. Spoon the vegetable mixture over the top and cover with the remaining potato wedges. Sprinkle the rest of the 4 cheeses over the top.

6 Cook in a preheated oven, 400°F/200°C for 30 minutes, or until the potatoes are cooked and the top is golden brown. Serve garnished with fresh thyme sprigs.

pan potato cake

serves four

1½ lb/675 g waxy potatoes, unpeeled and sliced

1 carrot, diced

8 oz/225 g small broccoli flowerets

5 tbsp butter

2 tbsp vegetable oil

1 red onion, cut into quarters

2 garlic cloves, crushed

6 oz/175 g firm bean curd, drained and diced

2 tbsp chopped fresh sage

¾ cup grated sharp cheese

1 Cook the sliced potatoes in a large pan of boiling water for 10 minutes. Drain thoroughly.

2 Meanwhile, cook the carrot and broccoli flowerets in a separate pan of boiling water for 5 minutes. Drain with a slotted spoon.

3 Heat the butter and oil in a 9-inch/ 2-cm skillet. Add the onion and garlic and cook over low heat for 2–3 minutes. Add half of the potato slices to the skillet, covering the base of the skillet.

4 Cover the potato slices with the carrot, broccoli, and the bean curd. Sprinkle with half of the sage and cover with the remaining potato slices. Sprinkle the grated cheese over the top.

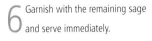

5 Cook over moderate heat for 8–10 minutes. Then place the pan under a preheated medium broiler for 2–3 minutes, or until the cheese melts and browns.

6 Garnish with the remaining sage and serve immediately.

bubble & squeak

serves four

2⅔ cups mealy diced potatoes

8 oz/225 g Savoy
    cabbage, shredded

5 tbsp vegetable oil

2 leeks, chopped

1 garlic clove, crushed

8 oz/225 g smoked bean
    curd, diced

salt and pepper

shredded cooked leek, to garnish

COOK'S TIP

This version is a perfect entrée, as the smoked bean curd cubes added to the basic bubble and squeak mixture make it very substantial and nourishing.

1 Cook the diced potatoes in a pan of lightly salted, boiling water for 10 minutes, until tender. Drain and mash the potatoes.

2 Meanwhile, in a separate pan, blanch the cabbage in boiling water for 5 minutes. Drain well and add to the potato.

3 Heat the oil in a heavy skillet. Add the leeks and garlic and cook gently for 2–3 minutes. Stir into the potato and cabbage mixture.

4 Add the smoked bean curd and season to taste with salt and pepper. Cook over medium heat for 10 minutes.

5 Carefully turn the whole mixture over and continue to cook over medium heat for 5–7 minutes more, or until crispy underneath.

6 Serve immediately, garnished with shredded leek.

potato-topped lentils

TOPPING

4 cups diced mealy potatoes

2 tbsp butter

1 tbsp milk

½ cup chopped pecan nuts

2 tbsp chopped fresh thyme

thyme sprigs, to garnish

FILLING

1 cup red lentils

5 tbsp cup butter

1 leek, sliced

2 garlic cloves, crushed

1 celery stalk, chopped

4½ oz/125 g broccoli flowerets

6 oz/175 g smoked bean curd, diced

2 tsp tomato paste

salt and pepper

COOK'S TIP

Bean curd is quite delicate, so always use a very sharp knife when dicing or slicing it. A blunt knife would crush it.

---

1 To make the topping, cook the potatoes in a pan of boiling water for 10–15 minutes, or until cooked through. Drain well. Add the butter and milk and mash thoroughly. Stir in the pecan nuts and chopped thyme and set aside.

2 Cook the lentils in boiling water for 20–30 minutes, or until tender. Drain and set aside.

3 Melt the butter in a skillet. Add the leek, garlic, celery, and broccoli. Cook over medium heat, stirring frequently, for 5 minutes, until softened. Add the bean curd cubes. Stir

VARIATION

You can use almost any combination of your favorite vegetables in this dish.

---

in the lentils, together with the tomato paste. Season with salt and pepper to taste, then turn the mixture into the base of a shallow ovenproof dish.

4 Spoon the mashed potato on top of the lentil mixture, spreading to cover it completely.

5 Cook in a preheated oven, 400°F/ 200°C, for about 30–35 minutes, or until the topping is golden brown. Garnish with sprigs of fresh thyme and serve hot.

cauliflower gratin

serves four

1 lb 2 oz/500 g cauliflower flowerets

1 lb 5 oz/600 g potatoes, diced

3½ oz/100 g cherry tomatoes

SAUCE

2 tbsp butter or margarine

1 leek, sliced

1 garlic clove, crushed

3 tbsp all-purpose flour

1¼ cups milk

¾ cup mixed grated cheese, such as
    sharp Cheddar, Parmesan, and
    Swiss cheese

½ tsp paprika

2 tbsp chopped fresh
    flatleaf parsley

salt and pepper

chopped fresh parsley,
    to garnish

1 Cook the cauliflower in a pan of boiling water for 10 minutes. Drain and reserve. Meanwhile, cook the potatoes in a pan of boiling water for 10 minutes, drain and reserve.

2 To make the sauce, melt the butter or margarine in a pan and sauté the leek and garlic for 1 minute. Stir in the flour and cook, stirring constantly, for 1 minute. Remove the pan from the heat and gradually stir in the milk, ½ cup of the cheese, the paprika, and the parsley. Return the pan to the heat and bring to a boil, stirring constantly. Season with salt and pepper to taste.

3 Spoon the cauliflower into a deep ovenproof dish. Add the cherry tomatoes and top with the potatoes. Pour the sauce over the potatoes and sprinkle on the remaining cheese.

4 Cook in a preheated oven, 350°F/180°C, for 20 minutes, or until the vegetables are cooked through and the cheese is golden brown and bubbling. Garnish and serve immediately.

nutty harvest loaf

serves four

2 tbsp butter, plus extra for greasing

2⅔ cups diced mealy potatoes

1 onion, chopped

2 garlic cloves, crushed

generous 1 cup unsalted peanuts

1⅓ cups fresh white bread crumbs

1 egg, beaten

2 tbsp chopped fresh cilantro

⅔ cup vegetable bouillon

generous 1 cup sliced mushrooms

1¾ oz/50 g sun-dried tomatoes in
    oil, drained and sliced

salt and pepper

SAUCE

⅔ cup sour cream

2 tsp tomato paste

2 tsp clear honey

2 tbsp chopped fresh cilantro

1 Grease a 1-lb/450-g loaf pan.
Cook the potatoes in a pan of boiling water for 10 minutes, until cooked through. Drain well, then mash and set aside.

2 Melt half of the butter in a skillet. Add the onion and garlic and cook gently for 2–3 minutes, until soft. Finely chop the nuts, or process them in a food processor for 30 seconds with the bread crumbs.

3 Mix the chopped nuts and bread crumbs into the potatoes with the egg, cilantro, and vegetable bouillon. Stir in the onion and garlic, season to taste, and mix well.

4 Melt the remaining butter in the skillet. Add the sliced mushrooms and cook for 2–3 minutes.

5 Press half of the potato mixture into the base of the loaf pan. Spoon the mushrooms on top and sprinkle with the sun-dried tomatoes. Spoon the remaining potato mixture on top and smooth the surface. Cover with aluminum foil and bake in a preheated oven, 350°F/190°C, for 1 hour, or until firm to the touch.

6 Meanwhile, mix the sauce ingredients together. Cut the nutty harvest loaf into slices and serve with the sauce.

potato & eggplant gratin

serves four

1 lb 2 oz/500 g waxy
   potatoes, sliced

1 tbsp vegetable oil

1 onion, chopped

2 garlic cloves, crushed

1 lb 2 oz/500 g firm bean
   curd, drained and diced

2 tbsp tomato paste

½ cup all-purpose flour

1¼ cups vegetable bouillon

2 large tomatoes, sliced

1 eggplant, sliced

2 tbsp chopped fresh thyme

scant 2 cups plain yogurt

2 eggs, beaten

salt and pepper

salad, to serve

VARIATION

You can use marinated or
smoked bean curd for extra
flavor, if you like.

1 Cook the sliced potatoes in a pan of boiling water for 10 minutes, until tender but not breaking up. Drain and then set aside.

2 Heat the oil in a skillet. Add the onion and garlic and cook, stirring occasionally, for 2–3 minutes.

3 Add the bean curd, tomato paste, and flour and cook for 1 minute. Gradually stir in the bouillon and bring to a boil, stirring. Reduce the heat and simmer for 10 minutes.

4 Arrange a layer of the potato slices in the base of a deep ovenproof dish. Spoon the bean curd mixture evenly on top. Layer the sliced tomatoes, then the eggplant, and finally, the remaining potato slices on top of the bean curd mixture, making sure that it is completely covered. Sprinkle with thyme.

5 Combine the yogurt and beaten eggs in a bowl and season to taste with salt and pepper. Spoon the yogurt topping over the sliced potatoes to cover them completely.

6 Bake in a preheated oven, 375°F/190°C, for about 35–45 minutes, or until the topping is browned. Serve with a crisp salad.

stuffed rice crêpes

COOK'S TIP

Specialist Indian flours, and
mustard and onion seeds, are
available from some large
supermarkets and from Indian
food stores.

1 To make the dosas, soak the rice
and urid dhal for 3 hours. Grind
the rice and urid dhal to a smooth
consistency, adding water if necessary.
Set aside for 3 hours more to ferment.
Alternatively, if you are using ground
rice and urid dhal flour (ata), combine
in a bowl. Add the water and salt and
stir until a batter is formed.

2 Heat about 1 tablespoon of oil in
a large, nonstick skillet. Using a
ladle, spoon the batter into the skillet.
Tilt the skillet to spread the mixture
over the base. Cover and cook over
medium heat for about 2 minutes.
Remove the lid and turn the dosa over
very carefully. Pour a little oil around
the edge, then cover and cook for
2 minutes more. Repeat with the
remaining batter.

3 To make the filling, cook the
potatoes in a pan of boiling
water. Add the green chiles, turmeric,
and salt, and cook until the potatoes
are just soft. Drain and mash lightly
with a fork.

4 Heat the vegetable oil in a pan
and cook the mustard and onion
seeds, dried red chiles, and curry
leaves, stirring constantly, for about
1 minute. Pour the spice mixture over
the mashed potatoes, then sprinkle
over the lemon juice and mix well.
Spoon the potato filling on one half of
each of the dosas and fold the other
half over it. Transfer to a warmed
serving dish, garnish and serve hot.

potato & vegetable curry

serves four

4 tbsp vegetable oil

1 lb 8 oz/675 g lb waxy potatoes,
  cut into large chunks

2 onions, cut into quarters

3 garlic cloves, crushed

1 tsp garam masala

½ tsp ground turmeric

½ tsp ground cumin

½ tsp ground coriander

2 tsp grated fresh gingerroot

1 fresh red chile, seeded
  and chopped

8 oz/225 g cauliflower flowerets

4 tomatoes, skinned and cut into
  fourths

¾ cup frozen peas

2 tbsp chopped fresh cilantro

1¼ cups vegetable bouillon

shredded cilantro, to garnish

boiled rice or Indian bread, to serve

COOK'S TIP

Using a large, heavy-based
pan or skillet for this recipe
ensures that the potatoes
are cooked thoroughly.

1 Heat the vegetable oil in a large heavy pan or skillet. Add the potato chunks, onion, and garlic and cook over low heat, stirring frequently, for 2–3 minutes.

2 Add the garam masala, turmeric, ground cumin, ground coriander, grated ginger, and chopped chile to the pan, mixing the spices into the vegetables. Cook over low heat, stirring constantly, for 1 minute.

3 Add the cauliflower flowerets, tomatoes, peas, chopped cilantro to the curry mixture and stir well to mix. Pour in the vegetable bouillon and stir again.

4 Cook the potato curry over low heat for 30–40 minutes, or until the potatoes are tender and completely cooked through.

5 Garnish the potato curry with fresh cilantro and serve with plain boiled rice or warm Indian bread.

garbanzo curry

serves four

6 tbsp vegetable oil

2 onions, sliced

1 tsp finely chopped fresh
   gingerroot

1 tsp ground cumin

1 tsp ground coriander

1 tsp crushed garlic

1 tsp chili powder

2 fresh green chiles

1tbsp fresh cilantro leaves

⅔ cup water

10½ oz/300 g potatoes

14 oz/400 g canned garbanzo
   beans, drained and rinsed

1 tbsp lemon or lime juice

chapatis, to serve (optional)

1 Heat the oil in a large pan over medium heat.

2 Add the onions to the pan and cook, stirring occasionally, until golden brown.

3 Reduce the heat, then add the ginger, ground cumin, ground coriander, garlic, chili powder, fresh green chiles, and fresh cilantro leaves to the pan and stir-fry for 2 minutes.

4 Add the water to the mixture in the pan and stir to mix.

5 Using a sharp knife, cut the potatoes into small dice.

6 Add the potatoes and the drained garbanzo beans to the mixture in the pan. Cover and simmer, stirring occasionally, for 5–7 minutes.

7 Sprinkle the lemon or lime juice over the curry.

8 Transfer the garbanzo bean curry to serving dishes. Serve the curry hot with chapatis, if you like.

potato curry

serves four

3 medium potatoes

⅔ cup vegetable oil

1 tsp onion seeds

½ tsp fennel seeds

4 curry leaves

1 tsp ground cumin

1 tsp ground coriander

1 tsp chili powder

pinch of ground turmeric

1 tsp salt

1½ tsp dried mango powder

1 Peel and rinse the potatoes. Using a sharp knife, cut each potato into 6 slices.

2 Cook the potato slices in a large pan of boiling water until just cooked, but not mushy (test by piercing with the point of a sharp knife or a skewer). Drain thoroughly and set aside until required.

3 Heat the vegetable oil in a separate, heavy pan over moderate heat. Reduce the heat to low and add the onion seeds, fennel seeds, and curry leaves and stir thoroughly.

4 Remove the pan from the heat and add the ground cumin, coriander, chili powder, turmeric, salt, and dried mango powder, stirring well to combine.

5 Return the pan to low heat and cook the mixture, stirring constantly, for about 1 minute.

6 Pour this mixture over the cooked potatoes, mix together, and stir-fry over low heat for about 5 minutes.

7 Transfer the potato curry to warm individual serving dishes and serve immediately.

vegetable pulao

serves six

2 potatoes, each cut into 12 pieces

1 eggplant, cut into 6 pieces

2 carrots, sliced

1¾ oz/50 g green beans, chopped

4 tbsp vegetable ghee

2 onions, sliced

¾ cup plain yogurt

2 tsp finely chopped fresh
  gingerroot

2 tsp crushed garlic

2 tsp garam masala

2 tsp black cumin seeds

½ tsp ground turmeric

3 black cardamom pods

3 cinnamon sticks

2 tsp salt

1 tsp chili powder

½ tsp saffron threads

1¼ cups milk

3 cups basmati rice

5 tbsp lemon juice

TO GARNISH

4 fresh green chiles, seeded
  and chopped

fresh cilantro leaves, chopped

1 Prepare the vegetables. Heat the ghee in a skillet. Add the potatoes, eggplant, carrots, and beans and cook, turning frequently, until softened. Remove from the pan and set aside.

2 Add the onions and cook, stirring frequently, until soft. Add the yogurt, ginger, garlic, garam masala, 1 teaspoon black cumin seeds, the turmeric, 1 cardamom pod, 1 cinnamon stick, 1 teaspoon salt, and the chili powder and cook for 3–5 minutes. Return the vegetables to the pan and cook for 4–5 minutes.

3 Put the saffron and milk in a small pan and bring to a boil, stirring constantly. Remove from the heat and set aside.

4 In a pan of boiling water, half-cook the rice with 1 teaspoon salt, 2 cinnamon sticks, 2 black cardamom pods, and 1 teaspoon black cumin seeds. Drain the rice, leaving half in the pan, while transferring the other half to a bowl. Pour the vegetable mixture on top of the rice in the pan. Pour half of the lemon juice and half of the saffron milk over the vegetables and rice, then cover with the remaining rice and pour the remaining lemon juice and saffron milk over the top.

5 Garnish with chopped chiles and fresh cilantro, then return to the heat, and cover. Cook over low heat for about 20 minutes. Serve the vegetable pulao immediately.

bean curd & vegetable stir-fry

serves four

1¼ cups diced potatoes

1 tbsp vegetable oil

1 red onion, sliced

8 oz/225 g firm bean curd, drained
   and diced

2 zucchini, diced

8 canned artichoke hearts, halved

⅔ cup bottled strained tomatoes

1 tbsp sweet chili sauce

1 tbsp soy sauce

1 tsp superfine sugar

2 tbsp chopped fresh basil

salt and pepper

1 Cook the potatoes in a pan of boiling water for 10 minutes. Drain thoroughly and set aside until required.

2 Heat the vegetable oil in a wok or large skillet and sauté the red onion for 2 minutes, until the onion has softened, stirring constantly.

3 Stir in the bean curd and zucchini and cook for 3–4 minutes, until they begin to brown slightly.

4 Add the cooked potatoes to the wok or skillet, stirring to mix.

5 Stir in the artichoke hearts, bottled strained tomatoes, sweet chili sauce, soy sauce, sugar, and basil.

6 Season to taste with salt and pepper and cook for 5 minutes more, stirring well.

7 Transfer the bean curd and vegetable stir-fry to serving dishes and serve immediately.

mixed vegetables

serves four

1¼ cups vegetable oil

1 tsp mustard seeds

1 tsp onion seeds

½ tsp white cumin seeds

3–4 curry leaves, chopped

1 lb/450 g onions, chopped finely

3 tomatoes, chopped

½ red and ½ green bell pepper,
   seeded and sliced

1 tsp finely chopped fresh gingerroot

1 tsp fresh garlic, crushed

1 tsp chili powder

¼ tsp ground turmeric

1 tsp salt

2 cups water

1 lb/450 g potatoes, cut into pieces

½ cauliflower, cut into
   small flowerets

4 carrots, sliced

3 fresh green chiles, seeded and
   chopped finely

1 tbsp fresh cilantro leaves

1 tbsp lemon juice

1 Heat the oil in a large pan. Add the mustard, onion, and white cumin seeds, and the curry leaves and cook until they turn a shade darker.

2 Add the onions to the pan and cook over medium heat until golden brown.

3 Add the tomatoes and bell peppers and cook for about 5 minutes.

4 Add the ginger, garlic, chili powder, turmeric, and salt and mix well.

5 Add 1¼ cups of the water. Cover and simmer for 10–12 minutes, stirring occasionally.

6 Add the potatoes, cauliflower, carrots, green chiles, and cilantro leaves and cook for about 5 minutes.

7 Add the remaining ⅔ cup of water and the lemon juice, stirring to combine. Cover and simmer for about 15 minutes, stirring occasionally.

8 Transfer the mixed vegetables to warm, individual serving plates and serve immediately.

potato & cauliflower curry

⅔ cup vegetable oil

½ tsp white cumin seeds

4 dried red chiles

2 onions, sliced

1 tsp finely chopped fresh
    gingerroot

1 tsp crushed garlic

1 tsp chili powder

1 tsp salt

pinch of ground turmeric

1lb 8 oz/675g potatoes, chopped

½ cauliflower, cut into flowerets

2 fresh green chiles (optional)

1 tbsp fresh cilantro leaves

⅔ cup water

COOK'S TIP

Ground ginger is no
substitute for the fresh root.
It is less aromatic and
flavorsome and cannot be
used in sautéed dishes, as
it burns easily at the high
temperatures required.

---

1 Heat the oil in a large, heavy pan.
Add the white cumin seeds and
dried red chiles to the pan, stirring to
mix thoroughly.

2 Add the onions to the pan and
cook over medium heat, stirring
occasionally, for about 5–8 minutes,
until golden brown.

3 Combine the ginger, garlic, chili
powder, salt, and turmeric. Add
the spice mixture to the onions and
cook for about 2 minutes.

4 Add the potatoes and cauliflower
to the pan and stir to coat
thoroughly with the spice mixture.
Reduce the heat to low and add the
green chiles, if using, cilantro leaves,
and water to the pan. Cover and
simmer for about 10–15 minutes,
until the vegetables are cooked
through and tender.

5 Transfer the potato and
cauliflower curry to warmed
serving plates and serve immediately.